W9-AMA-322

Australia

Australia

Revised Edition

BY ANN HEINRICHS

Enchantment of the World
Second Series

Children's Press®

A Division of Scholastic Inc.

NEW YORK   TORONTO   LONDON   AUCKLAND   SYDNEY
MEXICO CITY   NEW DELHI   HONG KONG
DANBURY, CONNECTICUT

DISCARD

PUBLIC LIBRARY
EAST ORANGE PUBLIC LIBRARY

E
j'994
J HEI

Frontispiece: Sleepy Bay at Freycinet National Park

Consultant: Alan Tidwell, Director, Center for Australian and New Zealand Studies, Edmund A. Walsh School of Foreign Service, Georgetown University, Washington, D.C.

Please note: All statistics are as up-to-date as possible at the time of publication.

Book production by Herman Adler

Library of Congress Cataloging-in-Publication Data

Heinrichs, Ann.
  Australia / by Ann Heinrichs. — Rev. ed.
      p. cm. — (Enchantment of the world. Second series)
  Includes bibliographical references and index.
ISBN-13: 978-0-516-24873-8
ISBN-10: 0-516-24873-1
  1. Australia—Juvenile literature. I. Title. II. Series.
  DU96.H45 2007
  994—dc22   2006017586

© 2007 by Ann Heinrichs.
All rights reserved. Published in 2007 by Children's Press, an imprint of Scholastic
Library Publishing. Published simultaneously in Canada.
Printed in the United States of America.

CHILDREN'S PRESS and associated logos are trademarks and/or registered
trademarks of Scholastic Library Publishing. SCHOLASTIC and associated logos
are trademarks and/or registered trademarks of Scholastic Inc.
1 2 3 4 5 6 7 8 9 10 R 16 15 14 13 12 11 10 09 08 07

36.00
3/13/07
NRN

6124476924

Australia

Contents

Cover photo:
Koalas

Uluru

Didgeridoo

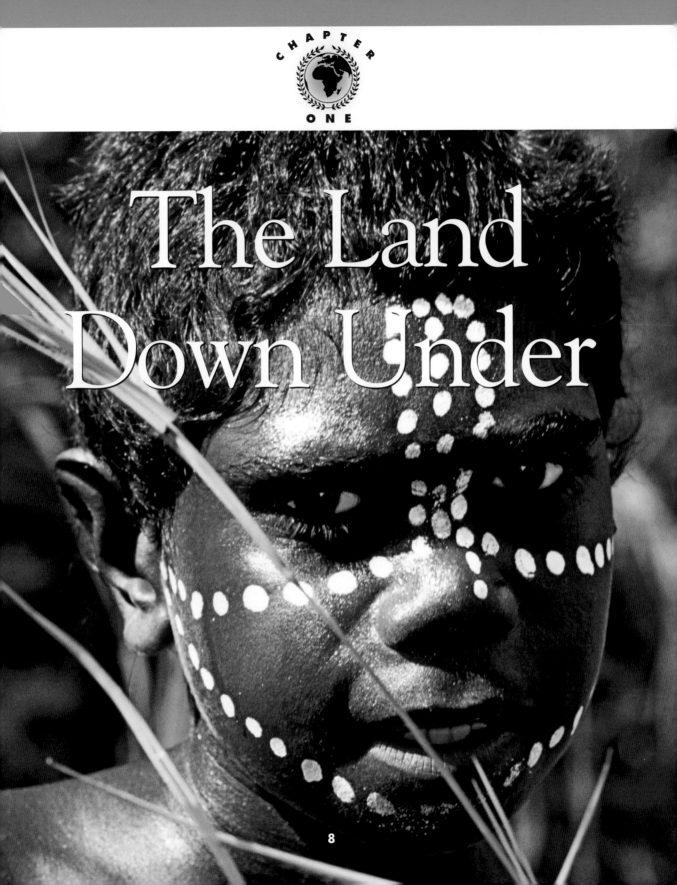

CHAPTER ONE

The Land Down Under

More than a thousand
Australian children attend
Schools of the Air.

SARAH LIVES IN THE OUTBACK. THAT'S THE VAST EXPANSE
of land in Australia's interior, away from the coastal cities.
She lives on a sheep station, or sheep ranch, that stretches
across thousands of acres. Like many outback kids, Sarah gets
her education from one of Australia's Schools of the Air—her
lessons are broadcast by satellite.

Sometimes Sarah joins her father on a mill run. They drive
around checking on the windmills that pump water from the
ground for the sheep to drink. Sarah helps out by cleaning the
water troughs. At sheepshearing time, she rides a motorcycle
or horse to help round up the sheep. On her drives around the
station, she often catches sight of kangaroos grazing or bounc-
ing across the fields.

Opposite: **Aborigines sometimes paint themselves with
symbols that are important
to them. Dots can mean
many things, including stars,
sparks, or the burnt earth.**

Kakadu National Park is managed jointly by its traditional Aboriginal owners and the Australian government.

Tarrah is an Australian Aborigine. She lives in Kakadu National Park, a lush part of Australia's Northern Territory, where her ancestors have lived for thousands of years. The Aborigines are the ancient people of Kakadu, and Tarrah's two grandmothers are elders of their clans. They teach her the tribal language, forgotten by so many over the years.

The grandmothers also teach Tarrah how to find "bush tucker"—food they get from the land. Tarrah knows the animals and plants that come and go as the seasons pass. She scans the muddy riverbanks, looking for long-necked turtles. She digs up water yams, with their large, fleshy roots. She also picks fruits and catches fish for bush tucker. As evening draws near, she hears the distant, lonely howl of a dingo, Australia's wild dog.

The Bush and the Outback

Australians call any wild place with trees or plants "the bush." "Going to the bush" also means leaving the city and going to the country. When someone goes all the way to the desert, then they're in "the outback."

Danny lives in Sydney, Australia's largest city. Dressed in his school uniform, he boards a train at 7:30 A.M. After crossing the Sydney Harbour Bridge, he arrives at school. Danny takes classes in English, math, science, and other standard subjects. When school is out at 3:00, he meets with his computer club, chess club, or school soccer team. Back at home, he feeds his pet mice and plays video games. On weekends, he heads for the beach, where he goes boogie boarding in the surf.

The Sydney Harbour Bridge is one of Sydney's most famous sites. It was the city's tallest structure until 1967.

These three kids represent some of the diverse cultures that thrive in Australia. Most of the country's population is clustered around the coastal cities. There, in the bustling centers of business and culture, people have all the advantages of modern city life. Between the coasts lies a vast expanse of bush, range, and desert. Farms, such as Sarah's sheep station, cover more than half the country. In mining regions, a day's drive might get you as far as one scraggly town.

AUSTRALIA

- ● Cities of over 100,000 people
- ○ Other cities
- ✪ National capital

0   500 miles

0   500 kilometers

INDONESIA

PAPUA NEW GUINEA

Arafura Sea

EAST TIMOR

INDIAN OCEAN

Darwin

Kakadu National Park

Weipa

Coral Sea

Wyndham

Derby

Broome

Purnululu National Park

Northern Territory

Cairns

Innisfail

Townsville

Great Barrier Reef Marine Park

Ayr

Bowen

Port Hedland

Dampier

Karijini National Park

Rudall River National Park

Tennant Creek

Mount Isa

Cloncurry

Queensland

Mackay

Exmouth

Western Australia

Alice Springs

Winton

Rockhampton

Gibson Desert Nature Reserve

Uluru National Park

Simpson Desert National Park

Gladstone

Carnarvon

Sturt National Park

Charleville

Maryborough

Kalbarri

Meekatharra

South Australia

Coober Pedy

Lake Eyre

Brisbane

Gold Coast

Geraldton

Kalgoorlie-Boulder

Nullarbor National Park

Bourke

Darling R.

Lismore

Port Macquarie

Perth

Merredin

Woomera

Lake Torrens

Dubbo

Newcastle

Rockingham

Bunbury

Nuytsland Nature Reserve

Esperance

Whyalla

New South Wales

Sydney

Gawler

Canberra ✪

Wollongong

Albany

Adelaide

Australian Capital Terr.

INDIAN OCEAN

N

W   E

S

Mount Gambier

Victoria

Geelong

Melbourne

Devonport

Launceston

Tasmania

Cradle Mountain-Lake St. Clair National Park

Hobart

Australia

For Australia's Aborigines, life in these desolate stretches comes naturally. They know their way around. For tens of thousands of years, they worked with a harsh climate and unforgiving land. They knew every plant, animal, and waterhole and taught their children the earth's secrets.

When white explorers arrived, a new era began. Australia would never be the same. Founded as a British prison colony, Australia grew into a thriving settlement of farms and mines. Its six separate colonies joined under a central government in 1901.

Australia has more kangaroos than it has people.

One of Australia's nicknames is "the Land Down Under"—down under the equator, that is. Because it lies in the Southern Hemisphere, its seasons are the opposite of those on the northern half of the globe. Danny's summer vacation from school begins in December!

For outsiders, Australia can cast an enchanting spell. Some see it as a land of cuddly koalas and bounding kangaroos. Others think it's a land of fearless bushmen like the knife-toting movie character Crocodile Dundee. But a typical Australian might say it's the land of footie and barbies—football and barbecues! As you explore Australia, you'll find that it's a fascinating blend of amazing facts and haunting legends.

An Island Continent

F

OR ANCIENT EUROPEANS, MOST OF THE KNOWN WORLD
lay in the Northern Hemisphere. Some people, however,
believed that the southern half of the Earth must hold vast
lands and civilizations, too. Around A.D. 150, the Greek
geographer Ptolemy drew a now-famous map of the world.
It included a great continent in the south. Ptolemy labeled
it *Terra Australis Incognita*—Latin for "Unknown Southern
Land." Australia eventually got its name from the Latin word
australis, meaning "southern."

Opposite: **Australia has 16,000 miles (25,760 km) of coastline.**

Ptolemy's famous map shows only three continents: Africa, Asia, and Europe.

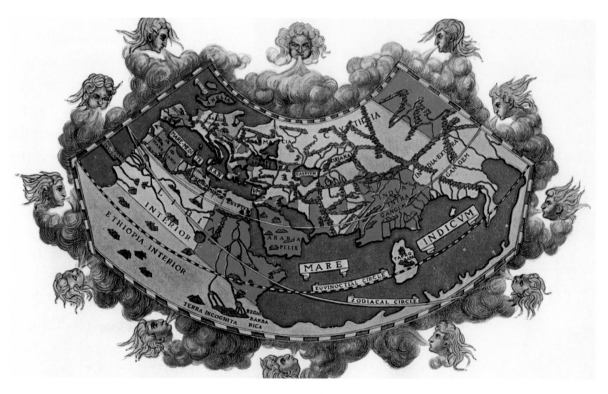

Australia is an island. To the east is a section of the Pacific Ocean called the Coral Sea, and to the west is the Indian Ocean. Australia is two islands, really. Tasmania, off the southeast coast, was once part of the mainland. Australia is not only a country, it's also a continent—the smallest of Earth's seven great landmasses.

Several other island nations are close to Australia. Just to the north are Papua New Guinea, Indonesia, and part of Malaysia. A little farther north are the Philippines and the Asian mainland. Southeast of Australia is New Zealand. To the south is the icy continent of Antarctica.

Australia's Cocos Islands lie in the middle of the Indian Ocean, 1,720 miles (2,768 km) northwest of Perth. No one lived on the islands until the early 1800s, when coconut farms were established there.

States and Territories

Australia is carved into six states and two mainland territories. Almost all their borders are perfectly straight, drawn along lines of latitude and longitude. It's easy to learn the layout of Australia. Western Australia covers the western one-third of the continent. Down the center are the Northern Territory and South Australia. The eastern third is Queensland, New South Wales, Victoria, and Tasmania. The tiny Australian Capital Territory is totally surrounded by New South Wales.

Australia's Geographic Features

Area: 2,978,146 square miles (7,713,364 sq km)

Greatest Distance, East–West: Almost 2,485 miles (4,000 km)

Greatest Distance, North–South: About 2,300 miles (3,700 km)

Highest Elevation: Mount Kosciusko, 7,310 feet (2,228 m)

Lowest Elevation: Lake Eyre, 52 feet (16 m) below sea level

Largest Lake: Lake Eyre (often dry)

Longest River: Darling River, 1,702 miles (2,739 km)

Largest Desert: Great Victoria Desert

Average January Temperatures: Sydney, 72°F (22°C) Darwin, 83°F (29°C)

Average July Temperatures: Sydney, 53°F (12°C) Darwin, 77°F (25°C)

Average Annual Rainfall: Sydney, 48 inches (122 cm) Darwin, 62 inches (157 cm)

Australia also claims several so-called external territories. Four of them have a population of zero: the Ashmore and Cartier Islands, the Heard and McDonald Islands, the Coral Sea Islands, and the Australian Antarctic Territory. About 360 people live on Christmas Island, and Norfolk Island has about 1,800 residents. About 600 people live on the Cocos (Keeling) Islands.

Western Queensland is a mix of mountains, forests, and rich farmland.

The Eastern Highlands

The eastern edge of Australia is the eastern highlands region, the nation's best farmland. The region runs all the way from northern Queensland's Cape York Peninsula to southern Tasmania. Before land was cleared for cities and farms, lush rain forests covered the eastern highlands. Some of these rain forests still stand in unsettled parts of the region.

Along the Pacific coast is a low plain with beaches and jagged cliffs. Australia's heaviest population centers are on the east and southeast coasts. They include Brisbane, Sydney, and Melbourne. Canberra, the capital, is slightly inland.

The eastern highlands is also called the Great Dividing Range. It's not really a mountain range, but a stretch of hills and plateaus covered with grasslands and forests. Australia's highest mountains—the Australian Alps—rise at the south end of the Great Dividing Range. Australians and tourists from around the world love to ski in the Snowy Mountains, the highest range in the Australian Alps. Australia's tallest peak, Mount Kosciusko, rises in the Snowies.

The island of Tasmania is part of the Great Dividing Range, too. A land bridge once connected it to the mainland. Now the Bass Strait flows between Australia and Tasmania. Southwestern Tasmania is a wilderness of rugged mountains, river rapids, and thundering waterfalls.

Beautiful Russell Falls cascades down a mountainside over three rocky steps. It is the most visited site in Tasmania's Mount Field National Park.

The Central Lowlands

Beyond the Great Dividing Range are the central lowlands. They extend from the Gulf of Carpentaria in the north to the southeast coast of South Australia. Rain falls in the far north and far south, but the lowlands are generally dry. Most crops cannot grow there, but cattle graze on the tough grass and scrubby shrubs.

The low, desolate Simpson Desert covers the western part of the lowlands, toward the center of the country. In northern South Australia, the dry beds of salt lakes stretch to the horizon. Among them is Lake Eyre, which is Australia's lowest point.

Flowers cling to a sand dune in the Simpson Desert. This desert is known for its red dunes.

Kakadu National Park

Kakadu National Park lies in what is called the Top End of the Northern Territory, on Australia's north-central coast. Kakadu is the largest national park in Australia and one of the largest in the world. Its name comes from Gagadju, the name of a local Aboriginal tribe. Aborigines have lived in this area for at least twenty-five thousand years. They lease Kakadu to the National Parks and Wildlife Service and take part in managing it.

Kakadu is famous for holding some ancient traces of Aboriginal life. Some rock paintings that adorn Nourlangie Rock, Ubirr Rock, and other park sites are more than twenty thousand years old. Kakadu is also renowned for the abundant life that populates its swamps and rain forests. Jabiru storks, crocodiles, and wallabies are among the thousands of species

of wildlife in the park. Much of the movie *Crocodile Dundee* was filmed in Kakadu.

The Western Plateau

The high, flat western plateau covers the western two-thirds of the country. Crops grow well in the far north and the southwest of this region because of plentiful rainfall. A low plain lines the seacoast. Herds of cattle and sheep graze farther inland, where the land is hilly and grassy. The region's biggest cities are seaports. Perth, in the southwest, is the largest of these.

Vast expanses of desert take up the central part of the plateau—the Great Victoria Desert in the south, the Gibson Desert in the center, and the Great Sandy Desert to the north. Farther north still is the Tanami Desert. At the Northern Territory's Top End are Arnhem Land and the city of Darwin. Along the southern coast is the Nullarbor Plain. *Nullarbor*

Wave Rock formed as wind and water wore away soft rock at the bottom, leaving behind an arc of harder rock.

means "no trees" in Latin, and it's a good name for this dry plateau. East of the plain, the city of Adelaide spreads out along a bay.

The western plateau is dotted with astounding rock formations. Smack in the middle of Australia is the massive red rock called Uluru, or Ayers Rock. East of Perth is a two-hundred-million-year-old rock formation called Wave Rock. Its arched shape and colorful granite stripes make it look like a giant wave. Deep gorges in vivid colors run through Karijini National Park in western Australia. In the northwest, the Bungle Bungle Range in Purnululu National Park features spectacular rock pillars, beehives, and domes.

The Shadowy Place

Uluru is a massive rock formation in the desolate center of Australia. An explorer named it Ayers Rock in 1873, after Henry Ayers, then chief secretary of South Australia. Iron oxide in the sandstone gives the rock its blazing, red-orange color. It rises 1,142 feet (348 m) above the surrounding desert, and a trek around its base is a 6-mile (10 km) hike.

Uluru, meaning "Shadowy Place," is sacred to the Aborigines, who ask visitors not to climb the rock. In 1985, the area was returned to the Pitjantjatjara Aborigines, its traditional owners, who live in the Aboriginal community of Mutitjulu, at the base of the rock. They jointly manage it with Australia's National Parks and Wildlife Service.

The Great Barrier Reef

Many a ship has been smashed to bits on the Great Barrier Reef. This string of rock-hard islands curves around Queensland's northeast coast for some 1,250 miles (2,000 kilometers). The surrounding waters are called the Coral Sea. Strangely enough, this reef—the scene of so much death and destruction—is made almost entirely of skeletons!

For millions of years, tiny sea creatures called coral polyps have lived off Australia's northeast coast. When a polyp dies, its skeleton remains on the ocean floor. Gradually, minerals in the seawater fill in the spaces where soft tissue had been. Over time, the skeletons become as hard as rock. With each new generation, living polyps attach themselves to the older, bony layers.

Layer after layer, the reef builds up until the highest mounds rise above the ocean surface. Spying the reef from afar, a sailor might think it's a patch of sandbars. But the visible part of the reef is only a fraction of the whole rocky mass. Even a slight collision can rip a gaping hole in a ship's hull.

The Great Barrier Reef is the world's largest coral reef. Scientists from around the world come to study its animal and plant life. Pollution and tourism have destroyed many other coral reefs, and the Great Barrier Reef is feeling the impact, too. The Australian government and international conservation agencies are working to preserve this natural treasure.

Climate

Almost half of Australia—the northern part of the country—lies in Earth's tropical zone. The tropics are a broad

Opposite: **The Great Barrier Reef is the largest structure on the planet built by living things.**

Heavy rains washed away a bridge in Bellingen, New South Wales, in 2006. The rains left three thousand people stranded.

band of land just north and south of the equator—an imaginary line around the Earth an equal distance from the two poles. Australia's tropical region is warm to hot all year. Weather in the far north is typical of the tropics, with a wet season (November to April) and a dry season (May to October). The southern part of the country has a temperate climate, with distinct seasons. Summers are warm, and winters are cold. Remember, though, that Australia lies in the Southern Hemisphere. July is midwinter for Australians, and January is midsummer!

Australia's vast desert regions are arid, with only rare rainfall. Australia's heaviest rains fall along the north, east, and southeast coasts. Queensland's coast is drenched with about 150 inches (380 centimeters) of rain every year. Snow is rare. Only the Australian Alps and parts of Tasmania get regular snowfalls.

The wet season brings violent rainstorms and cyclones on the north coast and floods farther inland. Droughts are common throughout much of Australia and can be devastating to the nation's economy. Crops shrivel and grasses die, leaving sheep and cattle without enough to eat. With the droughts come bushfires. These wildfires rage across millions of acres of land. The Canberra bushfires of 2003 damaged much of the Capital Territory. In South Australia, the Black Tuesday bushfire of 2005 was the country's most devastating fire in more than twenty years. Australia's expert fire service is working on more effective ways to handle bushfires.

Looking at Australia's State Capitals

Sydney, the capital of New South Wales, is Australia's oldest and largest city. Two of its most famous landmarks, the Sydney Opera House and Sydney Harbour Bridge, lie along Sydney Harbour. The bridge leads to the Rocks, where Australia's first settlers began their new life in 1788. That area is now Sydney's Old Town. The city center, Australia's economic hub, is built around Hyde Park. Looming over it all is Sydney Tower, with its high observation deck.

Melbourne (below), the capital of Victoria, grew up around the Yarra River. It is a mix of modern buildings and beautiful old structures from the mining boom of the 1850s. Its metropolitan area is huge, and much of it is devoted to gardens and parks. Melbourne is home to many European and Asian peoples—and their arts and food.

Brisbane (above), the capital of Queensland, straddles the Brisbane River. The city's Queensland Cultural Centre, a cluster of ultramodern buildings, stands alongside beautiful structures from earlier times, such as the Old Government House and the Post Office.

Perth, the capital of Western Australia, sits at the mouth of the Swan River on the Indian Ocean. Perth is the business and shipping center for the state's mining industries. Gleaming office buildings tower over the city center, while elegant old buildings line St. Georges Terrace. Perth's attractions include the Hay and Murray Street shopping malls and Kings Park, with its elevated walkway through the treetops.

Adelaide, the capital of South Australia, has been called the "city of churches." Today, modern high-rise buildings overshadow the early settlers' churches and stone houses. The River Torrens flows through Adelaide, and lush parks and gardens surround the city.

Hobart, the capital of Tasmania, is Australia's southernmost city. It sits at the foot of Mount Wellington, where the Derwent River meets the Tasman Sea. Hobart was an important whaling port in its early days. Old warehouses are now shops and restaurants along the cobblestone streets of Salamanca Place. The Tasmanian Museum and Art Gallery and the Maritime Museum cover the area's culture and history.

CHAPTER

THREE

Wild Things

SOME OF THE STRANGEST ANIMALS IN THE WORLD LIVE IN Australia. And many of them live nowhere but Australia. For instance, Australia is the only place on Earth where you find koalas and platypuses in the wild. This is due to the continent's geological history. At one time, Australia was connected to the other continents. Back then, its animals were much like those elsewhere in the world. When Australia broke away, its animals came with it. Separated from their relatives, they evolved in completely different ways.

Opposite: **Frilled lizards spend much of their lives in trees. They eat insects, spiders, and other lizards.**

Koalas live most of their lives in eucalyptus trees. They often stay in the same tree for days.

The National Animals

Australia's two national animals are the kangaroo and the emu. They appear on either side of the crest on Australia's national coat of arms. About fifty kinds of kangaroos live in Australia. The smallest is the rat kangaroo, which is about the size of a rab-

bit. The largest is the red kangaroo. It grows to be about 5 feet (1.5 m) tall. Large kangaroos can run up to 30 miles (50 km) an hour. In a running leap, they can jump 30 feet (9 m).

The emu is the world's second-largest bird, after the ostrich. It stands 5 to 6 feet (1.5 to 1.8 m) tall and weighs as much as 130 pounds (60 kg). Like kangaroos, emus can run up to 30 miles (50 km) an hour. They can swim, too. After the female lays her eggs, the male sits on them until they hatch.

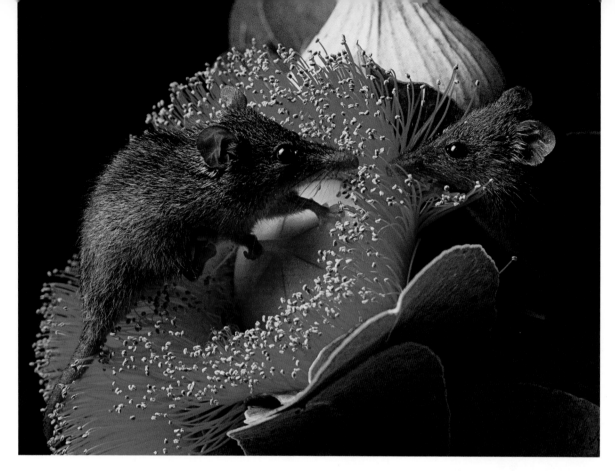

Honey possums are tiny, just 3 or 4 inches (8 or 10 cm) long, including the tail. They eat only the nectar and pollen from flowers.

Kangaroos, Koalas, and Other Marsupials

Kangaroos and koalas are probably the best-known Australian animals. Both are marsupials. These are animals that give birth to tiny young, which then grow in a pouch on the outside of the mother's body until they're ready to live on their own. A baby kangaroo, or joey, is only about 1 inch (2.5 cm) long at birth.

Australia is home to about 260 species of marsupials, including wallabies, moles, bandicoots, wombats, and possums. (*Possum* is the usual Australian word for *opossum*.) Wallabies are a type of kangaroo. They live on the open grasslands, while moles burrow into the desert sand. Bandicoots are small, ratlike creatures, and wombats look like little bears.

Koalas get most of the water they need from eucalyptus leaves, so they seldom drink water. In fact, the word *koala* is believed to come from an Aboriginal word that means "no drink."

Marsupials that walk and hop upright have their pouches on their bellies. These include kangaroos and wallabies. In climbing marsupials—such as koalas—the pouch is on the mother's back.

Koalas have a big, black, leathery nose; gray fur; and long claws for climbing trees. They spend most of their time up in eucalyptus trees, as their diet consists mostly of eucalyptus leaves. A koala eats as much as 3 pounds (1.4 kilograms) of leaves a day. To digest all that food, it sleeps in the fork of a tree for much of the day. A baby koala, also called a joey, lives in its mother's pouch for several months. After it comes out, it clings to its mother's back until it is almost a year old.

Mammals That Lay Eggs

Mammals are animals that have hair and give birth to fully formed baby animals. There are only two mammals in the world that lay eggs. They are called monotremes, and both are native to Australia. One is the platypus, which is sometimes called the duckbill. It has rich brown fur, a bill like a duck's, a tail like a beaver's, and webbed feet with claws. Its flat tail and webbed feet help it to swim.

Platypuses make their homes near rivers and streams. They hunt for food mostly at night, moving along the streambed to find worms, snails, and tiny water creatures. In the daytime,

Platypuses spend twelve hours a day looking for food. They sometimes eat half their own weight in a single day.

they burrow into the muddy riverbank and rest. In the spring, females build special nursery burrows. There they lay two eggs and curl around them to keep them warm until they hatch.

Australia's other monotreme is the echidna, or spiny ant-eater. The echidna looks a little like a porcupine, with long, prickly spines to protect it from predators. When in danger, an echidna may roll itself into a spiny ball. It may dig a hole with its sharp claws to hide under a log or in the ground. Echidnas have a long snout, and their long tongue shoots out to catch ants, termites, and other insects.

An echidna has a long, sticky tongue that can stretch 7 inches (17 cm) beyond its snout. This helps it reach into termite nests.

Dangerous Creatures

Some of Australia's most dangerous animals are reptiles. The crocodile that lives along the northern coast is a fearsome, meat-eating creature. It may grow 15 feet (4.5 meters) or longer. Its freshwater relative, however, poses no threat to humans. Measuring only about 8 feet (2.5 m), it feeds on water plants, fish, and other small water animals.

Australia's saltwater crocodile is the world's largest reptile.

Pythons, Australia's largest snakes, grow about 20 feet (6 m) long. They wrap themselves around their prey, squeeze it to death, and then swallow it whole. It may take days or even weeks for a python to digest an animal. Dogs, cattle, and even humans have fallen prey to pythons' deadly attacks. Reports from the bush tell of pythons that have died because a victim was simply too large to get through its digestive system.

In all, Australia has about 170 species of snake, and many of them are poisonous. Those with the deadliest venom are the taipan, the tiger snake, and the death adder.

Thorny devils look fearsome, but they are completely harmless.

Most of Australia's lizards are harmless, but they can look really scary. When the frilled lizard is alarmed, it unfurls its big fanlike collar, stands up on its hind legs, and prances away at high speed. Goannas get their name from a version of the word *iguana*, but they are actually monitor lizards. They range in length from 12 to 29 inches

Tasmanian devils have pale pink ears. When the creatures are excited or under stress, their ears turn dark red.

(30 to 74 cm) and may bite if they're annoyed. Thorny devils and geckos are other common Australian lizards.

Dingoes and Tasmanian Devils

The dingo is Australia's wild dog. Aborigines once tamed dingoes as pets, but today they're serious predators. Dingoes prey on sheep and other livestock, and they are sometimes bold enough to attack huge kangaroos. A dingo-proof barrier called the Wild Dog Fence ranks as the longest fence in the world. It stretches almost 3,300 miles (5,300 km) from southeast Queensland to South Australia's seacoast.

Tasmanian devils look cute on Saturday morning cartoons. But some say they're Australia's meanest, toughest animals. Their powerful bite inflicts an awful wound. They eat every last bit of their prey—bones, hair, and all. Tasmanian devils live only in Tasmania. They're nocturnal marsupials, feeding by night and sleeping by day.

Animal Imports

Europeans imported dozens of new animal species to Australia. Some were farm animals, such as sheep, cattle, and goats, but settlers also brought foxes, cats, and rabbits.

Rabbits arrived in Australia in the mid-1800s. They multiplied quickly, overrunning sheep and cattle pastures. Rabbit-proof fences helped a little, but farmers were only able to bring them under control by spreading a rabbit disease.

The Camels' Tale

Australia's first camel was named Harry. He arrived in a South Australian port in 1840. Harry was killed, though, after he bumped into his owner and caused a bad rifle accident. But many more camels were imported after that. These hardy pack animals could withstand long trips across Australia's deserts. By 1920, about twenty thousand camels had arrived from North Africa and the Middle East.

Camels were brought in to help explore and develop Australia's desert lands. They led explorers through the desert, pulled plows, and carted supplies for railroad-building crews. Thousands of camels were imported to work in Western Australia during the gold rush.

Some camels escaped into the wild. Explorers lost camels or left them behind. More and more camels were released in the 1920s and 1930s as motor vehicles took their place. Today, more than five hundred thousand camels roam Australia's deserts. Australia is now the only country where camels run wild.

Australia's camels eat grass, shrubs, tree leaves, and fruit. Adults need at least 4.2 ounces (119 grams) of salt a day, so camels are often seen around salt lakes. They sometimes crash through farmers' fences to get at watering troughs. Australia's agriculture department is looking for ways to put all these camels to good use.

Some settlers brought their pet cats to Australia. As litter after litter was born, the cats ran off and became feral, or wild. Now Australia's wild cats are serious predators, cutting down the populations of many birds and small mammals. Imported foxes became predators, too.

Cane toads came to Queensland in the 1930s. Farmers brought these "killer" toads from Hawaii to rid the sugarcane plantations of beetles. Moving on from the sugarcane fields, the toads multiplied in the wild. They're big enough to eat small animals, and their bodies contain a deadly poison that discourages predators.

In 1935, 102 cane toads were brought to Australia. Today, more than 100 million live in the country.

Birds

"Kookaburra sits in the old gum tree / Eating all the gum drops he can see." These are lines from an old song about one of Australia's most famous birds. Kookaburras are odd-looking relatives of the kingfisher. They have a thick, squat body and a thick bill. They're nicknamed "laughing jackasses" because of their loud, cackling call. The "gum drops" in the kookaburra song are drops of sap from a eucalyptus tree. Actually, kookaburras eat insects, lizards, mice, and snakes.

Hundreds of other bird species live in Australia. Emus and cassowaries are among the largest. Like ostriches, neither of these birds can fly. Another big bird is the jabiru, Australia's only stork. It's large and white with a glossy, dark-green head, neck, and tail.

In the tropical forests, brilliantly colored parrots and cockatoos screech and flit overhead. Lorikeets have bright red, blue, yellow, and green feathers. They are especially noisy. Parakeets, budgerigars, and zebra finches are other colorful—and noisy—species. They often travel in huge flocks.

The lyrebird is named for its long, gracefully curved plumes. The male's mating dance is spectacular, with its magnificent tail expanded and thrown forward over its head. The lyrebird inhabits the dense, damp forests of Australia's east coast. Occasionally, it uses its short wings for normal flight. But most of the time, a lyrebird takes flying jumps from rock to rock and tree to tree. The lyrebird was once hunted for its feathers. Today, it's a protected species.

Along the coast, familiar birds include cranes, ducks, geese, spoonbills, and pelicans. Australia is the only place in the world where black swans live. Dwarf penguins are found on the southern coast and in Tasmania.

Lorikeets are common in eastern Australia, even in the cities. They can often be seen in backyards, eating fruit off trees.

Colorful feather stars cling to coral in the Great Barrier Reef.

Life on the Great Barrier Reef

The Great Barrier Reef is alive with dazzling colors and bizarre shapes. More than fifteen hundred species of fish dart in and out of the coral. They include surgeonfish, butterfly fish, lionfish, angelfish, clown fish, and blue tangs. Groupers and sharks are among the large predators. About four hundred species of coral live there, too. Staghorn coral and brain coral look like their names. A brain coral can live for more than a hundred years.

Other reef residents are sea anemones, sea urchins, sea snails, lobsters, prawns, jellyfish, manta rays, and giant clams. There are also dugongs, large mammals similar to manatees.

Seabirds swoop over the coral islands and dive for fish, while herons and other shorebirds wade on the shallow banks. Sea turtles lay their eggs on some of the islands, too. Once hunted for food, the turtles are now protected.

A giant clam sits in front of soft corals. Giant clams weigh as much as 500 pounds (225 kg).

Termite Towers

The chunky brown towers that rise from the landscape in some desert regions are termite homes. Some of these termite towers are 20 feet (6 m) high. Termites build their towering nests by mixing soil and saliva.

Trees, Shrubs, and Grasses

Tall trees grow in dense rain forests on Australia's east coast and in the far southwest. Farther inland, trees are shorter and grow farther apart. They stand among low shrubs and grasses that are good for grazing. Deeper in the interior, scrubland is covered with tough-leaved bushes. As the land becomes more arid, the scrub becomes more sparse. A stiff, sharp-leaved grass called spinifex grows in some desert regions.

It's easy to tell when you're near a stand of eucalyptus trees—you can smell them. An oil on the leaves has a sharp, almost medicinal odor. The eucalyptus is the dominant tree of the continent. Australians call it the gum tree.

Eucalyptus trees can be found all over Australia, from desert to rain forest.

More than five hundred species of eucalyptus grow in Australia. In the rain forests, eucalyptus trees grow as high as 200 feet (60 m). Shrub species grow in the dryer scrublands. The locals call them mallee. Acacias, which Australians call wattles, are common plants in the interior. Australia is home to several hundred wattle species.

The National Floral Emblem

The golden wattle, a type of acacia, is Australia's national floral emblem. It's a golden-blossomed shrub or small tree that grows in the forest underbrush and scrublands of southeastern Australia. Golden wattles appear on Australia's coat of arms and on many postage stamps. On September 1, National Wattle Day, people are encouraged to plant an acacia.

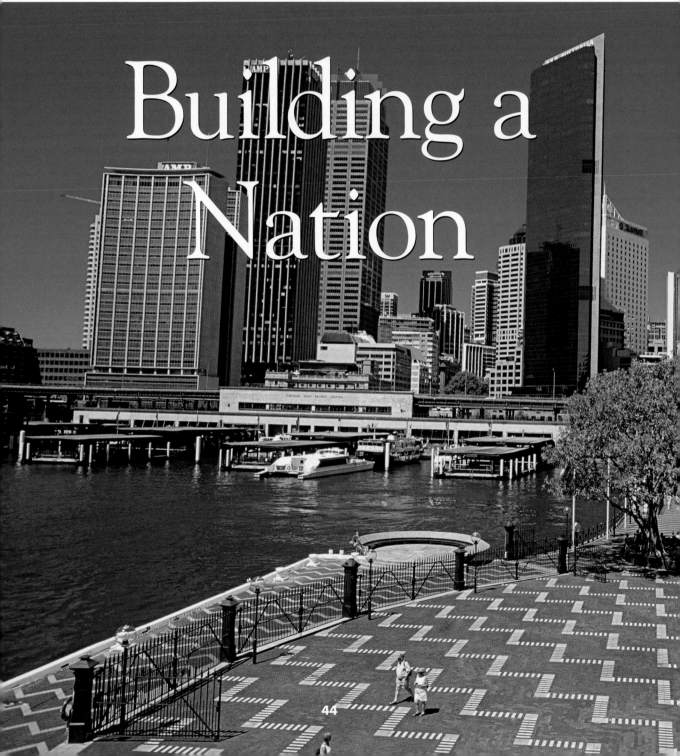

Building a Nation

HUMANS FIRST ARRIVED IN AUSTRALIA AT LEAST 40,000 years ago. Some experts believe they arrived as far back as 125,000 years ago. The first people in Australia migrated from Southeast Asia, either by boat or over land bridges. These people were the ancestors of Australia's Aborigines. By about 30,000 years ago, they had spread throughout the continent and the island of Tasmania.

Before Europeans arrived, between 250,000 and 1 million Aborigines lived in Australia. They lived in tribal settlements scattered over the continent. Each tribe was made up of clans of several families. The Aborigines hunted animals and gathered plants to eat. They ate roots and fruit, as well as kangaroos, possums, lizards, fish, and shellfish. They made tools and weapons of stones, bones, and shells. They also used millstones to grind grain. When wild game thinned out in one area, a clan moved to another spot.

Spiritual beliefs guided the Aborigines' way of life. They believed that mythical beings created the world and bestowed power. These beings belonged to a spiritual realm called the Dreaming, or the Dreamtime. Through

Opposite: **Sydney, Australia's largest city, is home to nearly 4.2 million people.**

Aborigines sometimes used a spear thrower called a woomera. The woomera enabled a person to throw a spear a greater distance.

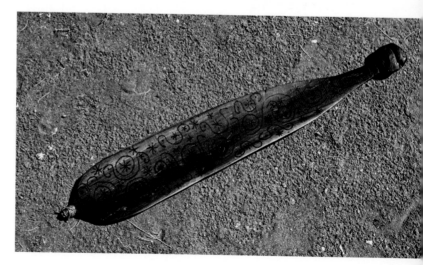

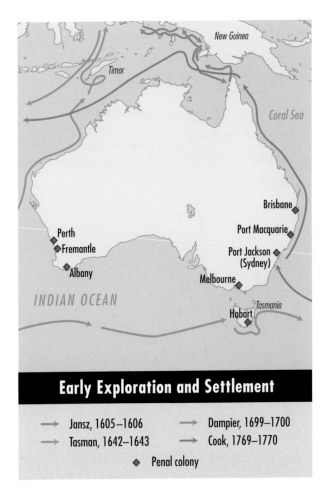

Early Exploration and Settlement

→ Jansz, 1605–1606 → Dampier, 1699–1700
→ Tasman, 1642–1643 → Cook, 1769–1770
◆ Penal colony

dances and rituals, the Aborigines kept in touch with the Dreaming beings and thus gained strength and wisdom.

The First Europeans

Willem Jansz, a Dutch navigator, was the first European to reach Australia. In 1606, he sailed along what is now Cape York Peninsula in northeast Australia. Jansz had no idea he had found the mysterious southern continent. At the time, he thought he was near a southern part of New Guinea, an island to the north of Australia.

Dutch seamen on a ship named the *Arnhem* explored Australia's northern coast in 1623 and named the area Arnhem Land—a name that is still used today.

Another Dutchman, Abel Janszoon Tasman, was sure he had found Ptolemy's "Unknown Southern Land." In 1642, he sailed from Indonesia on the orders of Antonij Van Diemen, governor of the region's Dutch colonies. Tasman rounded a point of land that he named Van Diemen's Land. Today, that land is the island of Tasmania.

William Dampier is credited with being the first Englishman to set foot in Australia. His ship, the *Cygnet*, beached in northwestern Australia in 1688. Dampier returned in 1699 to explore the west coast.

Captain Cook

Captain James Cook (1728–1779) of the British Royal Navy made several voyages of discovery. He explored North America's St. Lawrence River in 1759 and later mapped the coasts of Newfoundland and Labrador, in what is now Canada. In 1769, he led an expedition to the South Pacific island of Tahiti and then mapped the coasts of New Zealand, Australia, and New Guinea. On August 22, 1770, Cook claimed eastern Australia for England. Then he returned home, having sailed around the whole globe. On a later voyage, Cook completed another trip around the earth. He was killed by Hawaiian natives on a third attempt to circle the globe.

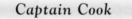

Captain Cook

Great Britain's Royal Navy sent Captain James Cook on a secret mission to find and claim the southern continent. In 1770, he sailed his ship *Endeavour* into a bay on Australia's east coast. With him was the botanist, or plant scientist, Sir Joseph Banks. Banks was so dazzled by the marvelous plant life that he named the place Botany Bay.

Cook continued exploring up the coast, naming land features as he went. After four months, he had claimed all of eastern Australia for King George III of Great Britain. He named it New South Wales.

At the time, Great Britain's jails were bursting at the seams. One way to relieve this problem was to send shiploads of prisoners out to the British colonies. But, in 1783, the

Captain Arthur Phillip inspects the first convicts sent to Australia. Between 1788 and 1868, about 162,000 convicts arrived in Australia.

American colonies had fought their way to independence. That left Britain with too many prisoners and nowhere to put them. New South Wales was the perfect solution.

The First Colony

In 1787, Captain Arthur Phillip set sail from England with a fleet of eleven ships. On board were about 780 convicts. One-fifth of them were women. They were to form the backbone of the new prison colony. About 200 British soldiers came along to keep them in line. Some soldiers brought their wives and children, too.

Phillip landed at Botany Bay on January 18, 1788. On January 26, a few miles up the coast, he and his passengers began their new life at Sydney Cove. Now the city of Sydney, this was the first European settlement in Australia. Australians now celebrate January 26 as National Day.

Other penal colonies followed. Convicts cleared and farmed the land and built houses and buildings for the colonial government. When a convict's term was up, he or she was set free. Until then, discipline was severe. Some convicts couldn't stand to wait until their sentences were done. Lucky escapees disappeared into the bush and were never found. Some became bushrangers, or outlaws.

Freed convicts and military officers were given land to farm. Many of them raised sheep and exported the wool to England. By law, the colonial government owned all of Australia's wide-open spaces. But the law couldn't stop farmers who were hungry for more land. Some, called squatters, simply moved onto a piece of land and began farming it. In time, they became some of Australia's biggest landowners.

Ned Kelly, Bushranger

Some of Australia's bushrangers were escaped convicts, while others were outlaws on the run. Because they robbed the rich and defied authority, bushrangers became folk heroes. They were celebrated in songs that told of their brave and daring deeds.

The most famous bushranger was Ned Kelly. He was known for robbing banks and having shoot-outs with police. In one shoot-out, he wore a suit of armor to fend off bullets. Ned had a kindly side, too. He fiercely protected his mother and siblings, and he once saved a drowning boy. Ned was finally captured in 1880. Although thousands of Australians signed a petition for mercy, he was hanged.

New explorations led to an influx of new settlers. Explorers reached Adelaide, on the southern coast, in 1830. South Australia became a British colony in 1836, with Adelaide as its capital. Settlers also arrived on the west coast and started the colony of Western Australia.

In New South Wales, sheep farming was becoming a big business. Always looking for bigger and better pastures, farmers opened up grazing lands south of the Murray River. That region became the colony of Victoria in 1851. The northern part of New South Wales became the colony of Queensland in 1859. Meanwhile, the little island called Van Diemen's Land held some of Australia's most infamous prisons. The island's name was officially changed to Tasmania in 1856.

In 1860 and 1861, Robert Burke and William Wills became the first white people to trek all the way across the continent from south to north. The two adventurers starved to death on the way back. Many other explorers met similar fates or simply disappeared without a trace.

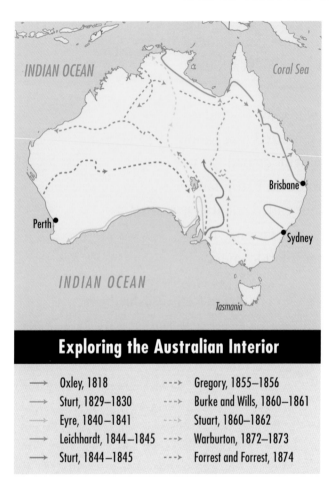

Exploring the Australian Interior

→ Oxley, 1818	⇢ Gregory, 1855–1856
→ Sturt, 1829–1830	⇢ Burke and Wills, 1860–1861
→ Eyre, 1840–1841	⇢ Stuart, 1860–1862
→ Leichhardt, 1844–1845	⇢ Warburton, 1872–1873
→ Sturt, 1844–1845	⇢ Forrest and Forrest, 1874

The Last of Her People

Tasmanian Aborigines lived farther south on earth than any other people. They died out in the 1800s, mainly from battling white settlers and becoming infected with their diseases. A woman named Truganini, believed to have been the last full-blooded Tasmanian Aborigine, died in 1876. Until 1976, her skeleton was in a Hobart museum. Then, in line with her own wishes, her remains were cremated and her ashes scattered off the southern Tasmania coast. The Truganini Reserve, just outside of Hobart, is named for her.

In the ten years before Burke and Wills made their trip, Australia's population almost tripled, from 400,000 to 1.1 million. As settlers took over more land, they pushed the Aborigines off their own homelands. Those who fought back were shot. Thousands of Aborigines were killed in these clashes. Diseases brought by settlers killed thousands more.

The Gold Rush

One day in the 1890s, a preacher's wife in Arizona got a rude surprise. On the kitchen table was a note from her husband saying he had taken off for Australia to dig for gold.

Gold had been discovered in New South Wales and Victoria in 1851. In the following decades, more gold was found in Queensland and the Northern Territory. The gold finds in Australia were huge. The famous "Holtermann nugget" weighed about 630 pounds

Australian troops rose to the challenge again in World War II (1939–1945). In North Africa, they successfully defended the city of Tobruk, Libya, from the Germans. Australians also played a decisive role in the battle of El Alamein, Egypt, in 1942.

Before that, however, the war arrived at Australia's back door. Fighting broke out in the Pacific region when Japan bombed the U.S. naval base at Pearl Harbor, Hawaii, in December 1941. In February 1942, Japan bombed the Northern Territory's capital of Darwin. U.S. general Douglas MacArthur set up headquarters in Australia, and the two countries fought together in many Pacific campaigns.

As before, the war boosted Australia's economy. The nation's factories turned out ammunition, airplanes, machine parts, and chemicals. Industries welcomed both men and women as workers. Cities swelled as people from the bush moved in for jobs.

Embracing the Wider World

After the war, Australia relaxed its immigration policy. Refugees from war-torn Europe began to arrive, adding a multicultural flavor to the larger cities. War in Southeast Asia brought another wave of immigrants in the 1970s, and the old White Australia policy was abandoned altogether in 1973.

Australia also increased trade with Asian nations. Japan, Taiwan, Singapore, Malaysia, Indonesia, and other countries along the Pacific Ocean became important trade partners.

Today, Australia enjoys one of the world's healthiest economies and highest standards of living. It continues to face many challenges, though. The 1990s brought drought and raging wildfires. Millions of acres of forest and grazing land were destroyed. In 1993, Aborigines won the right to make claims to tribal lands taken from them. Opposition has been fierce, as farmers and miners fear the loss of their holdings.

A wave of excitement swept the country when Sydney was chosen as the site of the Summer Olympic Games for the year 2000. The Games brought billions of dollars into Australia's economy.

But new concerns have also arisen in recent years. In 2002, terrorist bombs on the resort island of Bali, Indonesia, killed eighty-eight Australian tourists. In 2003, Australian troops joined the United States in a war to oust Saddam Hussein, the leader of Iraq. The following year, another bomb exploded outside the Australian embassy in Jakarta, Indonesia. Despite occasional tensions, Australia remains committed to fostering good relations with its international neighbors.

Tourists pass the site of a bomb blast on Bali in 2002. More than two hundred people were killed when two bombs exploded in a popular nightclub area.

Political
Australia

AUSTRALIA'S OFFICIAL NAME IS THE COMMONWEALTH of Australia. Though few people think of Australia as a monarchy, its form of government is actually a constitutional monarchy. That means that it has a monarch—a king or a queen—but the monarch's role is limited. When Australia became a nation in 1901, it kept some ties to the United Kingdom. Queen Elizabeth II of the United Kingdom is also the queen of Australia and Australia's head of state. Her representative in Australia is the governor-general. Both roles are mainly ceremonial, though.

The government of Australia is similar to the U.S. government in some ways and to Great Britain's government in other

Opposite: **A fountain shoots water above Lake Burley Griffin in Canberra, Australia's capital. The fountain was built in 1970 to honor the two-hundredth anniversary of Captain James Cook first landing in Australia.**

The Australian National Flag

Australia's national flag features a deep-blue background with the United Kingdom's flag in the upper

left-hand corner. Beneath that is a seven-pointed white star known as the Commonwealth Star. Six points of the star stand for Australia's six states, while the seventh point represents the Northern Territory, other territories, and any future states. On the right are the five stars that make up the Southern Cross. This constellation, visible in the Southern Hemisphere, has been a symbol for Australia and New Zealand since the 1700s. Australia adopted its flag in 1901.

Canberra: Did You Know This?

Canberra, the nation's capital, is the main part of the Australian Capital Territory. Lake Burley Griffin, named after Canberra's designer, cuts the city in half. The main government buildings are on the lake's south side, within the Parliamentary Triangle. The southernmost point of the triangle is the Parliament House on Capital Hill. Two legs of the triangle extend from this point and cross the lake—Commonwealth Avenue and Kings Avenue. Other buildings on the south side are the High Court building, the National Library, and the National Gallery of Australia.

Canberra's business section lies north of the lake. Its center is City Hill, in Vernon Circle. A tree-lined boulevard called Anzac Parade leads to the Australian War Memorial (above). This massive monument is the second-most-visited site in the country, after the Sydney Opera House. It honors Australia's role in wars from 1860 to the present.

Canberra was founded in 1913, twelve years after the federal government began, but it took many years to plan and build the city. Parliament held its first session in Canberra in 1927, and the new Parliament House opened in 1988.

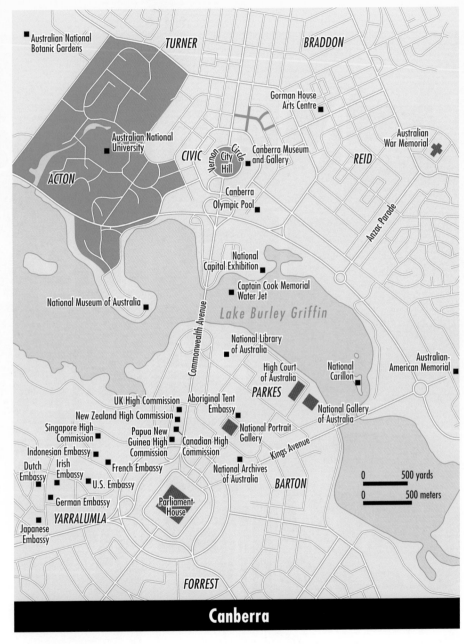

Canberra

Making a Living

In Australia, sheep and cattle roam the grasslands of the outback. Jackaroos, or ranch hands, tend the herds, either on horseback or on motorcycles. There are female ranch hands, too. They're called jillaroos! Some farmers have started to take in tourists to bring in needed income during hard times.

Opposite: **Trams ply the streets of Melbourne.**

Jackaroos heard cattle across the Mitchell River in Victoria.

Sheep and Cattle Stations

The British who founded the prison colony in Australia in 1788 brought sheep with them. Now Australia's sheep population is second only to the flocks in China. New South Wales and Western Australia are the country's top sheep-raising states. About four out of five sheep in Australia are merinos, which are bred for their heavy wool fleece. Australia is the world's largest producer of wool, followed by New Zealand and China. More than one-fourth of the world's wool is produced in Australia. The country is also a top exporter of mutton and lamb meat.

Sheepshearing time is the year's biggest event on a sheep

Merino sheep are the most common sheep in Australia. They are prized for their extremely soft wool.

station. The shearers use electric clippers to shave the fleece off the sheep. They try to remove it in one single piece. One large sheep can yield as much as 15 pounds (6.8 kg) of fleece.

Australian cattle are lean because they're pasture-fed rather than grain-fed. They get lots of exercise, and they don't live on fattening grains. Their meat has a much lower fat content

About 5,500 Australians make a living shearing sheep. An expert can shear a sheep in less than two minutes.

A New Way to Shear Sheep

Around the year 2000, a new method was introduced in Australia for removing the fleece from sheep. Called Bioclip, it involves injecting the sheep with a protein that causes it to shed its fleece. Bioclip removes more fleece than hand shearing. It also eliminates the stress and accidental cuts that shearing causes both sheep and shearer. Bioclip is meeting with some resistance, though, as sheepshearing is a long-held tradition in Australia.

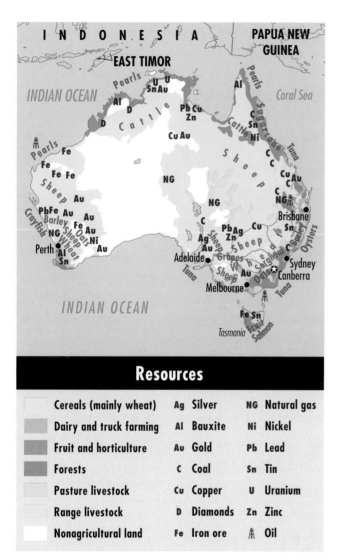

Resources

	Cereals (mainly wheat)	Ag	Silver	NG	Natural gas
	Dairy and truck farming	Al	Bauxite	Ni	Nickel
	Fruit and horticulture	Au	Gold	Pb	Lead
	Forests	C	Coal	Sn	Tin
	Pasture livestock	Cu	Copper	U	Uranium
	Range livestock	D	Diamonds	Zn	Zinc
	Nonagricultural land	Fe	Iron ore	⚒	Oil

than U.S. beef. Queensland and New South Wales are the leading cattle states. In north and central Australia, the land is so dry that a herd needs an immense grazing area to get enough to eat. Some cattle stations there are the size of small European countries.

Crops: In Second Place

Farming activities take up about 60 percent of Australia's total land area. About two-thirds of this land is used for grazing, while the rest is planted in crops. More than half the nation's farmland is in two states—Queensland and New South Wales.

Wheat is Australia's most important grain crop, followed by barley, oats, and sorghum. Sugarcane is also grown and processed into sugar, and the stalks and leaves are crushed to make animal feed. Potatoes, tomatoes, and carrots are Australia's main vegetable crops.

Grapes, oranges, apples, and bananas are the major fruit crops. The grapes are made into fine wines for local use and export. Pears, peaches, mangoes, melons, and pineapples are also produced.

The National Gemstone

The opal was proclaimed Australia's national gemstone in 1993. Often called "fire of the desert," opals glisten with flashing colors. An Aboriginal legend says that opals were created when a rainbow fell to the earth. About 95 percent of the world's precious opals come from Australia.

Mining

Almost all the opals in the world come from Australia. The country is a top diamond producer, too. But precious stones take second place to Australia's valuable minerals. Australia is the world's largest producer of bauxite and one of the top producers of uranium, iron ore, zinc, and nickel.

Gold hunters overran Western Australia in the 1890s. Now that state produces most of Australia's crude oil, iron ore, nickel, and gold; all the country's liquid natural gas; and almost all of its diamonds. Queensland is the leading producer of bauxite, copper, and silver, while New South Wales leads in coal, lead, and zinc. Every year,

Reddish colored stockpiles of red iron ore are abundant in Western Australia. Australia exports more iron ore than any other country in the world.

People wait for trains in the Perth Railway Station.

Afghan Railway, named for these camel drivers, runs along an old camel route between Adelaide and Alice Springs. Since 2003, the line—called Ghan for short—has continued north to Darwin for a full north–south trip across the continent.

The Ghan is one of Australia's luxury trains for long-distance travel. Another is the Queenslander, which runs from Brisbane to Cairns. But the nation's longest trip of all is on the Indian Pacific Railway. It crosses the entire width of the country, from Perth on the west coast to Sydney on the east, and takes three days.

Most of Australia's railroads haul farm and mining products into port cities along the coast. Western Australia's iron mines, for instance, rely heavily on freight trains.

Subways and commuter trains serve passengers in Sydney and Melbourne. Several cities used to have trams, or electric cable cars that run on city streets. Today, only Melbourne still has a major tram system.

Roads and railroads tend to radiate out from Australia's large port cities and state capitals. This pattern developed in the 1800s, when the colony depended mainly on trade with Great Britain. Today, national highways run between the state capitals. Paved roads reach many of the larger cities in the interior, too. For most of the outback, though, dirt roads are the rule.

Traveling in the dry and deserted outback can be dangerous. Drivers should always carry lots of water and always make sure someone else knows their travel plans.

Faces from Many Places

AUSTRALIA COUNTS ALL ITS PEOPLE EVERY FIVE years. In the 2001 census, the nation had almost 19 million people. In 2006, the population was about 20.6 million.

If Australians were spread out evenly across the country, there would be only seven people on every square mile (three per sq km) of land. In reality, though, Australians are spread out very unevenly. About four out of five residents live in the southeastern part of the country, and most of those live in the large coastal cities. Only 4 percent of Australians live in the outback, which covers 80 percent of the nation's land area.

To many outsiders, Australia conjures up romantic images of life in the outback. But most Australians are city dwellers. About 85 percent of the people live in urban areas.

Opposite: **Australians are among the world's healthiest people. They live an average of eighty years.**

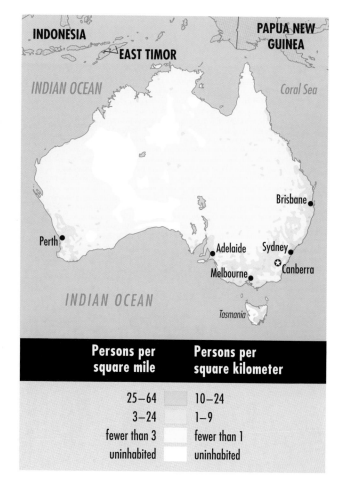

Persons per square mile	Persons per square kilometer
25–64	10–24
3–24	1–9
fewer than 3	fewer than 1
uninhabited	uninhabited

A Multicultural Nation

In its early days, Australia needed newcomers to help settle the land and provide labor. Most of the people admitted to the country then were

People crowd the streets of Melbourne for a parade marking Greek Independence Day.

English, Scottish, and Irish. Others, such as the Chinese who came to work during the gold rush, were urged to leave when their labor was no longer needed. When Australia became a nation in 1901, this attitude continued with the new government's White Australia policy.

After World War II, Australia began to welcome immigrants from other nations. Many came from Italy, Greece, and the Netherlands. Today, Melbourne is home to the largest Greek community outside of Greece itself. Other immigrants came from Lebanon, central Europe, and South America.

In the 1970s, refugees from Vietnam, Laos, Cambodia, and other Southeast Asian nations poured in. They were fleeing the war and upheaval that plagued the region. By 1973, Australia had removed all barriers to immigration on the basis of race. Today, most new Australian immigrants are Asians. Australia now prides itself on its multicultural makeup.

More than one-fifth of the people in Australia today were born overseas. The largest groups of foreign-born residents came from the United Kingdom, New Zealand, and Italy. Others arrived from Ireland and other European nations. Newcomers from North Africa and the Middle East include many Arabic-speaking people as well as Turks, Kurds, and Iranians. Australia's Asian immigrants were born in lands such as China, Hong Kong, Macao, and Malaysia.

Little Bourke Street is the center of Melbourne's Chinatown. Chinese people first moved to the city during the gold rush of the 1850s.

Ethnic Australia

English	33.9%
Irish	10.2%
Other European	22.1%
Asian	7.1%
Aborigines and Torres Strait Islanders	2.2%
Middle Eastern	1.9%
Other	22.6%

Native Land Claims

Beginning in 1893, Aboriginal reserves were set aside for Australia's native peoples. But those areas are small compared with the Aborigines' original territory—the whole continent. The 1976 Aboriginal Land Rights Act was a big step toward correcting the imbalance. This act, which related only to the Northern Territory, was the first Australian law to spell out a basis for Aboriginal land claims. It said Aborigines could make claims on land if they could prove they had a continuous link to that land since before Europeans arrived.

The landmark Native Title Act of 1993 gave indigenous, or native, Australians the right to make land claims in the nation's courts. Actually, it was a lawsuit by Torres Strait Islander Eddie Mabo that led to the new policy. Mabo's case established that Australia was never uninhabited and that indigenous people had a preexisting right to their land before white settlers came. The *Wik* decision of 1996 gave equal

Eddie Mabo

Eddie Koiki Mabo (1936–1992) was a community leader and human rights activist. He was born on Mer, also called Murray Island, one of the Torres Strait Islands. In his early life, Mabo worked as a pearl fisher and a railroad worker. Then he got a job as a gardener at James Cook University in Townsville, Queensland. While he was there, he sat in on class lectures, read library books, and had discussions with professors.

Mabo was shocked to learn that the government owned his native island. In 1988, Mabo brought a lawsuit against Queensland, arguing that the island's residents owned their land. He lost the case but appealed the decision to the High Court of Australia. Mabo died in January 1992, five months before the court issued a landmark ruling in his favor. For the first time, the court recognized that indigenous land ownership existed in Australia before Europeans arrived.

land rights to indigenous people and other Australians grazing animals on the same piece of land.

Each of these measures has been a step toward restoring what was taken from Aborigines. Many laws come with conditions that also whittle away at Aboriginal land rights. Australia's lawmakers continue to try and strike a balance between acknowledging indigenous land rights and giving back the whole country.

Australia is home to nearly half a million Aborigines. About 30 percent live in major cities. while the rest live in smaller towns and more remote areas.

Speaking Australian: Common Words and Phrases

Austraian	American
barbie	barbecue
bikie	motorcycle rider
billabong	a water hole in a dry riverbed
bloke	man
boomer	kangaroo
bunyip	mythical spirit animal of the bush
chemist's	drugstore
fair dinkum	really, honestly
g'day	hello
jumbuck	sheep
jumper	sweater
lollies	candy, sweets
mate	buddy, pal
never-never	the very remote outback
Oz	Australia
sunbake	sunbathe
walkabout	a long, rambling trip
water biscuit	cracker
wog	the flu
wowser	spoilsport
yobbo	a thug or uncouth person

Language

English arrived in Australia with the island's first British settlers. Over time, the accent and vocabulary have gone through some changes. For example, the Australian long *a* sound approaches the sound of an American long *i*. Thus, "mate" tends to be pronounced "mite," and "day" as "die." So the typical Australian greeting "G'day, mate" sounds more like "G'die, mite!" Australians call their dialect Strine. That's a shortened version of "Australian" ("Aus-trine"). They call themselves Aussies, and they call their country Oz (as in "Oz-tralia").

Many British terms are used in Australian English, such as *lift* (elevator), *petrol* (gasoline), and *telly* (television). Early settlers added new words for unfamiliar plants and animals, and in some cases, they picked up Aboriginal words. Aboriginal words that made their way into English include boomerang, kangaroo, koala, wallaby, and wombat.

Aboriginal languages are not related to any other languages outside the country. Several hundred Aboriginal dialects, or versions of languages, existed before Europeans arrived. Most of them disappeared as their native speakers died out. Only about two hundred Aboriginal languages still exist. Fewer

The Human Development Index

Every year, the United Nations ranks the countries of the world in terms of life expectancy, education level, income, health conditions, and many other factors. Each country is then given an overall rank on the Human Development Index. The 2005 index ranked Australia third among the 177 countries surveyed. Norway was first, and Iceland was second. Canada was fifth, while the United States was tenth.

than twenty of those are still used regularly, and they, too, are endangered. Other languages live on only in the memories of the elderly.

Today, only about one out of seven Aborigines can speak their native language. But there is a revival of ethnic pride among Aborigines, and Aboriginal cultural groups are working to preserve their languages. They meet with older people who may be the last surviving speakers of a dying language. After collecting information on the language, they teach others to speak it.

The Tiwi Islands, off the coast from Darwin, are home to a thriving Aboriginal community. Most people on the islands can speak the Tiwi language.

Children in Australia are well educated. A good indication of that is the country's literacy rate. That's the percentage of the population over fifteen years of age who can read and write. Australia's literacy rate is higher than 99 percent. In the United States, the literacy rate is about 97 percent.

About two-thirds of school-age children attend free public schools. Each state and territory operates its own school system, using funds from the federal government. Most of Australia's private schools are run by the Roman Catholic Church. The national government also provides some support to private schools.

Most children in Australia wear uniforms to school.

Each state and territory sets its own dates for the school term. Since Australia's seasons are the reverse of those in the Northern Hemisphere, summer vacation usually runs from mid-December through January. The school year usually begins in early February. In some states, kids have a two-week break two or three times a year. In most areas, children begin a preparatory year of school at age five, followed by six or seven years of primary school. Secondary school begins at age twelve and lasts another five or six years. Most students who finish secondary school go on to college.

Australia's first colleges were the University of Sydney (founded in 1850) and the University of Melbourne (1853). Today, the country has close to forty colleges and universities.

The University of Sydney was established in 1850. Many of its early buildings were inspired by Oxford University in England.

Opposite: **Students attending Schools of the Air spend about thirty minutes a day on the radio with their teacher. They spend another five or six hours working on lessons at home.**

For years, the regular public-school system overlooked Aboriginal children. A new policy, begun in 1989, aims to extend public education to Aborigines. Special programs now teach students about Aboriginal culture, too. Most Aboriginal children attend primary school in towns, on sheep or cattle stations, or over the radio. For secondary school, they may attend a boarding school or take correspondence courses. But many don't go beyond primary education.

Schools of the Air

Children in the outback live far away from regular schools. They get an education through a unique Australian invention—Schools of the Air. In this system, students in their homes communicate with teachers at faraway broadcast stations via shortwave radio. The teachers are specially trained to run a "classroom" over the airwaves.

The first School of the Air opened in 1951 in Alice Springs. After that, more than a dozen Schools of the Air opened throughout the outback, serving more than a thousand students. Several students can tune in at once.

Beginning with the 2003 school year, some schools began using new technology. They switched from radio to satellite. This allows students to take virtual classes in which they can see their teachers on their computer screens. Through each student's web camera, the teachers can see the students, too. Students can also hear their classmates and take part in group discussions and even schoolwide assemblies.

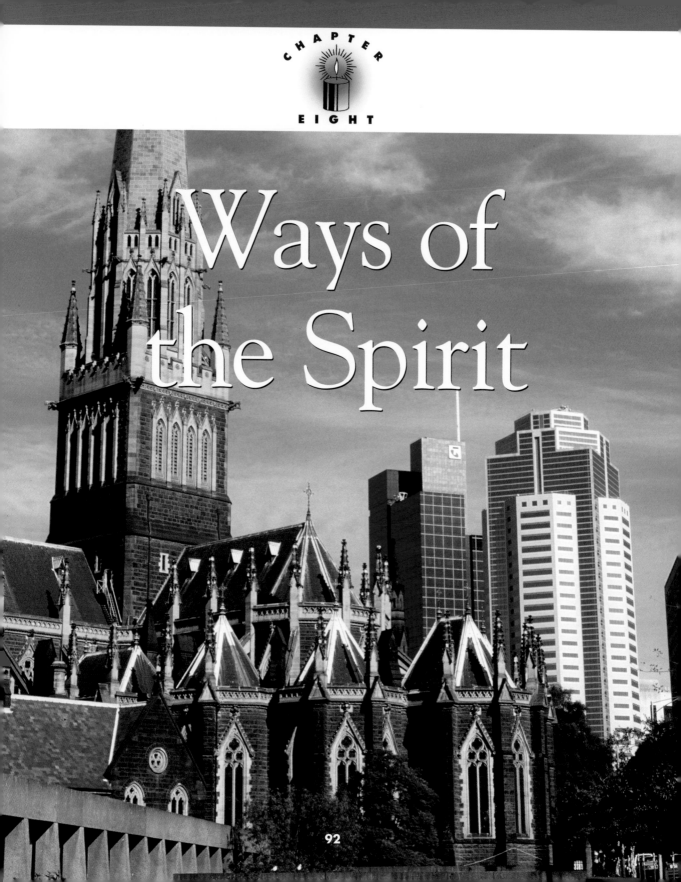

Ways of the Spirit

It's sometimes said that "no religion" is Australia's major religion. In the 2001 census, a full 27 percent of the population claimed to have no religion or didn't answer the religion question at all. But religion has played a central role in Australia's history, and freedom of religion is a cornerstone of Australia's constitution.

Opposite: **St. Patrick's Cathedral is the center of the Roman Catholic Church in Melbourne.**

Construction began on St. Paul's Cathedral in Melbourne in 1885. It was built on the site of the first Christian service in Melbourne.

Christianity

In colonial times, most white Australians belonged to the Church of England, or Anglican Church. Irish immigrants brought Roman Catholicism to Australia, and Catholic immigrants from Italy and Asia added to their numbers.

Anglicans and Catholics are still Australia's largest Christian groups. The Uniting Church is another large religious group. It was formed in 1977 when most of the country's Methodists, Presbyterians, and Congregationalists merged into one church. Other Christians in Australia today include Baptists, Lutherans, Pentecostals, and members of the Churches of Christ.

Roman Catholics have lived in Australia for more than two hundred years. They are now the largest religious group in the country.

A Broad Religious Mix

After World War II, waves of immigrants brought different religions into the country. Most of Australia's large Greek community belong to the Greek Orthodox Church. The number of Buddhists in Australia has risen since the 1970s, as more and more Asians have arrived from Vietnam, Laos, Thailand, and Tibet.

Buddhism is the fastest growing religion in Australia. Many Australian Buddhists immigrated from Vietnam, China, Cambodia, and Thailand. This Buddist temple is in Bendigo, Victoria.

Camel drivers brought the religion of Islam to Australia in the 1800s. Whites called the camel drivers Afghans, but many were from Pakistan and India. Today, Muslims—followers of Islam—are a fast-growing religious group in Australia. Many newcomers from the Middle East and South Asia are Muslims. Today, about three hundred thousand Muslims live in Australia.

Muslims in Australia come from more than sixty different ethnic groups. Most people who attend Sydney's Auburn Gallipoli Mosque are of Turkish descent.

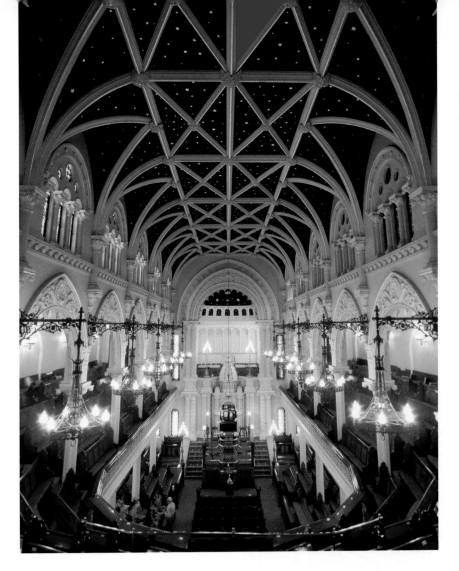

The Great Synagogue in Sydney opened in 1878. It is the most famous Jewish building in Australia.

Jewish people were among the first settlers to sail to Australia in 1788. Today, Australia's Jewish community numbers about eighty-four thousand. The Great Synagogue in Sydney is the country's major Jewish house of worship.

Religions in Australia*

Roman Catholic	26.6%
Anglican	20.7%
Other Christians	20.7%
Non-Christian religions (Buddhism, Islam, Hinduism, Judaism, other)	4.9%
No religion	15.5%
Not stated/inadequately described	11.7%

*Figures do not add up to 100% because of rounding.

The Dreaming

Before Europeans arrived, Aborigines enjoyed a rich, free-flowing spiritual life. Daily activities and the world of nature were charged with the life of the spirit.

The Dreaming, or Dreamtime, is central to the Aborigines' belief system. The Dreaming is the spiritual realm that existed long before the world began. Spirit beings of the Dreaming created the land and all plants, animals, and humans. They set down the laws of nature and the rules for orderly living. Then they were absorbed into the landscape. Dreamtime beings continue to energize all of nature and serve as the guiding force in everyday life.

Each Aboriginal clan honors its own totems. Totems are symbols such as plants, animals, ancestors, or Dreaming beings. An animal totem stood for all the powerful qualities of that species. Natural sites such as hills or rock formations could also be totems. In Aboriginal

This bark painting shows a group of spirit beings.

belief, a spiritual creature may have transformed itself into one of these landforms. Through their totems, people kept in touch with nature and with the Dreaming.

Religious rituals were a vital part of Aboriginal life. People spent weeks planning and preparing for a ceremony. Some rituals were complex dances with music and chants. Performers were often adorned with body paint and headdresses. Artists made bark paintings and carved wooden totems to use in ceremonies, too. For an Aboriginal boy, an important ritual was his initiation into the secrets of adult male life. Women and girls had their own secret rituals, too.

As Aborigines lost their land, they lost touch with their religion and culture. "If you take our land," said an elder of Arnhem Land, "you take our soul."

The Bull Roarer

Aboriginal men and women often held their own ceremonies. An instrument called a bull roarer was used in men's ceremonies. A bull roarer is a piece of wood tied to the end of a cord. When swung in the air, it makes a deep, loud, moaning sound. When Aboriginal women and children heard the moan of a bull roarer, they knew a ceremony was in progress and they should stay away.

Arts and Sports

AUSTRALIA HAS PRODUCED MANY ENTERTAINERS who are famous around the world. Actors Nicole Kidman, Russell Crowe, and Cate Blanchett have become superstars. Wildlife conservationist and television personality Steve Irwin was known internationally as the Crocodile Hunter. Irwin, with his wife Terri, owned the Australia Zoo in Beerwah, Queensland. In 2006, Irwin died tragically when a stingray spine pierced his chest while he was snorkeling off the Great Barrier Reef, filming a documentary. Director Peter Weir gained worldwide attention with *Picnic at Hanging Rock* (1975) and *Gallipoli* (1981), a movie about World War I. Bruce Beresford's *Breaker Morant* came out in 1980. Director George Miller made *Mad Max* (1979) and *The Road Warrior* (1981). *Strictly Ballroom*, *Muriel's Wedding*, and *Shine* are some other popular Australian films.

Opposite: **An Aborigine plays a didgeridoo.**

Cate Blanchett won an Academy Award for her role in *The Aviator*.

Nicole Kidman

Nicole Kidman was born in Hawaii in 1967. Her parents were Australian, and the family moved back to Australia when Nicole was four. In her teens, she began appearing in Australian movies and TV series. Her first American film was *Days of Thunder*, costarring actor Tom Cruise. Kidman and Cruise were married in 1990 and divorced in 2001. Meanwhile, Kidman's career grew. She received the 2003 Academy Award for best actress for her role in *The Hours*. Her other films include *To Die For* (1995), *Moulin Rouge* (2001), *Cold Mountain* (2003), and *Stepford Wives* (2004).

Since 1994, Kidman has been a goodwill ambassador for the United Nations Children's Fund (UNICEF), an international organization that seeks to improve the health and welfare of children around the world. In 2006, she was made a Companion of the Order of Australia, the country's highest civilian honor, for her acting accomplishments and her charitable work.

Russell Crowe

Russell Crowe was born in New Zealand in 1964 and moved to Australia at age four. He dropped out of secondary school to help support his family. While in his twenties, Crowe began acting in an Australian TV soap opera. Then he moved on to films. He received an Academy Award for best actor for his work in *Gladiator* (2000). His performances in *The Insider* (1999) and *A Beautiful Mind* (2001) also earned him Academy Award nominations. Crowe is part owner of an Australian rugby team and also performs with a rock band.

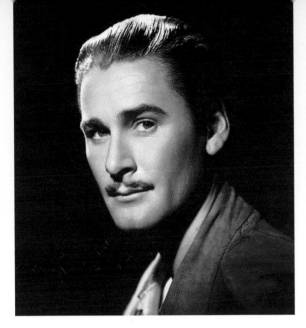

Errol Flynn

Errol Flynn (1909–1959) was a wildly popular Hollywood actor of the 1930s and 1940s. Born in Hobart, Tasmania, Flynn was a mischievous child. He recalled that his mother used to call him a "wicked, wicked boy." On screen, Flynn portrayed a romantic hero and a swash-buckling adventurer. Among his more than sixty movies are *The Adventures of Robin Hood, Captain Blood, The Sea Hawk, They Died with Their Boots On,* and *The Sun Also Rises.*

Australia has also produced many popular rock bands. They include AC/DC, Men at Work, INXS, and Midnight Oil. All these bands started out in Australian music clubs, then went on to worldwide fame. Young people in Australia today hear the latest pop music on radio and TV and in clubs. Pop concerts in the cities draw huge crowds, just as they do in Europe and the Americas.

INXS was one of the world's most popular bands in the late 1980s and early 1990s.

Some famous classical musicians have come out of Australia, too. Composer Percy Grainger (1882–1961) wrote charming versions of British folk tunes. Nellie Melba was an international opera star in the 1890s. Another opera singer, Dame Joan Sutherland, began to catch the world's attention in the 1960s.

The Australia Council for the Arts, a government agency, supports the national Opera Australia and the Australian Ballet. It also supports hundreds of other cultural groups and arts festivals throughout the country. Audiences fill the massive Sydney Opera House for operas, ballets, and plays, as well as orchestra and chamber music concerts.

The Sydney Dance Company is Australia's more renowned modern dance company. It is famed for its intense creativity and broad range of styles.

Each state capital has its own symphony orchestra, managed by the Australian Broadcasting Corporation (ABC). The ABC also broadcasts the orchestras' concerts and features international music stars in concerts. Each state is proud of its own opera and dance companies. The Australian Ballet, the Sydney Dance Company, and the Victoria State Opera have all enjoyed successful tours in other countries.

The Sydney Opera House

Ask any non-Australian to name a famous building in Australia, and they'll probably pick the Sydney Opera House. This massive arts complex is the busiest arts center in the world. More than one hundred million people have visited it since it opened in 1973. With its soaring, pointed arches looming over Sydney Harbour, it's a stunning piece of modern architecture. The Opera Theatre and 2,700-seat Concert Hall are just two of the many spaces in the opera house. Others are rehearsal studios, dressing rooms, restaurants, bars, and reception halls.

Dance ceremonies played an important part in traditional Aboriginal culture. Today, groups such as the Tjapukai Dance Theatre give performances that provide a window into that culture.

Aboriginal Music and Dance

For the Aborigines, music and dance are centuries-old rituals. Some dances mimic the movements of animals, while others tell ancient myths and spiritual tales. The Aboriginal Islander Dance Theatre performs many types of traditional Aboriginal music and dance.

A wooden tube called a didgeridoo is a traditional Aboriginal instrument. Music makers may beat out rhythms with sticks, clubs, or boomerangs or beat on an animal skin stretched over a frame. Tribes traditionally described their territory through songs, instead of maps. Aboriginal songs include sacred chants with hundreds of verses. There are songs that describe a journey, tell a clan's history, or lament the dead. Simple songs for entertainment may consist only of short verses or repeated phrases. Music and dance are an important part of *corroborees*, the Aborigines' group get-togethers.

Painting Traditions

Early Aboriginal people painted with ochre, a reddish-orange mineral that they ground up and mixed with water. They painted everyday scenes or sacred, mythical figures on tree bark, wood, and rock. Typically, the figures were drawn in "X-ray" style, showing their bones and inner organs. Some paintings discovered on cave walls and rock faces are twenty-five thousand years old.

Ancient Aboriginal paintings adorn the walls of several caves near Kimberley, in northwestern Australia.

Today, Aboriginal artists produce beautiful paintings in their traditional style. Aboriginal children are learning their native art traditions, too. In school and community programs, artists teach them the ancient techniques and symbols. Storytelling is an important part of the process. As the artists work, they tell stories about the creatures they're painting and what they mean.

In the 1800s, Australian artists painted in the impressionist style, which was popular in Europe at the time. In the late 1800s, a group of these artists became known as the Heidelberg school—the name of the Melbourne suburb where they worked. Their paintings showed shimmering, haunting landscapes and rural scenes.

Clifford Possum Tjapaltjarri

Clifford Possum Tjapaltjarri (c. 1932–2002) was one of Australia's most famous Aboriginal artists. A member of the Anmatyerre tribe, Possum was born in the desert of central Australia and spent years working on cattle stations. His early artworks were wood carvings. Later, in Papunya in the Northern Territory, an art teacher encouraged him and other Aborigines to put their Dreamtime stories on canvas. This led to the Papunya Tula painting style, sometimes called "dot art." Possum, the most famous Papunya Tula painter, captured a wealth of Aboriginal culture in his vivid paintings. He died the day he was to be appointed an Officer of the Order of Australia, a civilian honor for contribution to the arts.

Some of Australia's greatest modern painters are Russell Drysdale, Sidney Nolan, and Frederick Williams. Nolan painted fantastic scenes from Australian folklore. Drysdale and Williams specialized in scenes of the outback.

With government funding for the arts, many cities have built excellent art museums. Australia's national art museum is the National Gallery of Australia in Canberra. It includes a large collection of Australian art along with masterpieces from around the world.

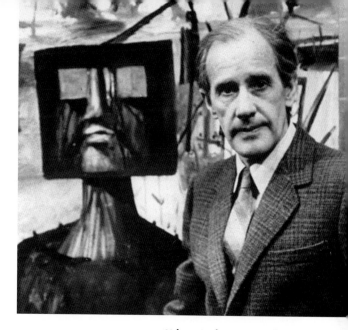

Sidney Nolan is considered the greatest Australian artist of the twentieth century. He is most famous for a series of paintings about the life of outlaw Ned Kelly.

Literature

During Australia's early years as a colony, many Europeans liked to read about its exotic landscapes and wildlife. They devoured the writings of Australian explorers and naturalists. The first Australian novel, published in 1830, was *Quintus Servinton*, about the life of a convict. The author, Henry Savery, was a convict himself. The same theme runs through Marcus Clarke's powerful novel *His Natural Life* (1874). It tells the wretched story of a convict in an Australian prison colony.

In the late 1800s, life in the Australian bush was a common subject. "Bush ballads" and short stories about bush life were published in the weekly *Bulletin*, called the "bushman's bible." Some of its finest pieces were bush stories by Henry Lawson and the ballad "Waltzing Matilda," by Andrew Barton "The Banjo" Paterson.

Waltz of the Banjo Man

Andrew Barton Paterson (1864–1941) was born in Narambla, New South Wales. He was a lawyer, a newspaper reporter, the editor of the *Sydney Evening News*, and a World War I ambulance driver. Paterson published his first poetry collection, *The Man from Snowy River and Other Verses*, in 1895. He signed his poems "The Banjo."

Paterson is best known and loved for his bush ballad "Waltzing Matilda," which became an unofficial Australian anthem. It tells the tale of a swagman (wandering laborer) sitting by a billabong (water hole) heating up his billy (tea) over the campfire, singing, "You'll come a-waltzing, Matilda, with me." Along came a jumbuck (sheep), and he stuck it in his tucker-bag (food sack). Then came a squatter (sheep farmer) with troopers to arrest him. The swagman swore they'd never take him alive. Into the billabong he sprang, singing, "You'll come a-waltzing, Matilda, with me." And if you pass by, they say, you can still hear him sing.

Patrick White has been called the greatest modern Australian writer. His novels, which include *The Tree of Man*, *Voss*, and *Riders in the Chariot*, deal with the complex emotions of often isolated people. White won the Nobel Prize for Literature in 1973.

Novelist Thomas Keneally was interested in the way one individual can affect great events in history. His novels include *The Chant of Jimmie Blacksmith* (1972) and *Schindler's Ark* (1982). When it was published in the United States, *Schindler's Ark* was retitled *Schindler's List*. It was the basis for Stephen Spielberg's haunting 1993 film.

Thomas Keneally is best known for his novels about real figures from history.

Sports

Most Australians learn to love sports at an early age and never outgrow their sports fever. Every town has amateur sports teams, and fans crowd the stadiums to cheer their favorite professionals.

Australian Rules Football, or "footie," is uniquely Australian. The first game took place in Melbourne in 1858. The Grand Final—like the Super Bowl in the United States—is one of the biggest sports events of the year. Footie is played on a huge field with eighteen players on each team. Players kick or hit the ball to advance it downfield. They can also run with it, though they

Austra tennis, ar dates bac including and Rod
The ming, s is the r ers and hosts also e back

Australian Rules Football was invented in Melbourne in 1858. A cricket player named Tom Wills developed it as a way to keep in shape during the winter.

Cathy Freeman

Track star Cathy Freeman is one of Australia's most popular athletes. Born in Mackay, Queensland, in 1973, she won her first race in a school event at age eight. As an Aborigine, Freeman was denied many privileges and honors as her athletic skills grew, but she just kept on running. Eventually, she became the first Aboriginal track star to represent Australia in the Olympic Games. In the 1996 Olympics in Atlanta, Georgia, Freeman won the silver medal in the 400-meter race. At the 2000 Olympics in Sydney, she was chosen to light the Olympic flame during the opening ceremonies. To the delight of her fans, she went on to win the gold medal in the 400-meter event. For her victory lap, she circled the track with both the Australian and the Aboriginal flag.

How People Live

Evo

Tennis legend
Aborigine, w
Wales. As a
racist comm
believed in
A strong p
with little e
times, the
Open onc

Double Bay is one of Sydney's wealthiest suburbs.

THE VAST MAJORITY OF AUSTRALIANS LIVE IN URBAN areas. But life in Australia is a bit different from life in many big cities around the world. City dwellers in Australia have more living space. They don't have to live in tightly packed high-rise apartment buildings.

Residential parts of Australian cities are called suburbs, and they look much like suburbs in other countries. Most people live in a single-family house with a yard. Typically, there's a barbie (barbecue grill) in the backyard. Even in the city, wildlife is never far away. Snakes, possums, and lizards are likely to drop by.

Opposite: **Peaceful, relaxing spots abound in Australia.**

Farming and mining are the main activities in the outback. For hardworking miners, the mining towns offer stores for their basic needs. Then there's the town pub. It's a much-needed place for friendship, storytelling, and bragging about a bright future.

Sheep and cattle stations, like mines, are usually a long drive from the nearest town. Ranchers might drive into town once a week to pick up food and supplies and take care of any business. Cattle roundups and sheepshearing are the high points of the year.

Many Australian miners do not live where they work. They fly into remote areas and work for two or three weeks and then fly home for a week off.

The Caves of Coober Pedy

Coober Pedy is a mining town in South Australia. It lies in the heart of the outback, hundreds of miles from the state capital of Adelaide. Most of the world's opals are mined in this area, and the miners and other residents live in cave houses built into the mountainsides or underground. Their homes are spacious, comfortable, and cool. It may be 113°F (45°C) outside, but inside the cave houses, it's a cool 73°F (23°C).

Kids in the outback have lots of space for roaming around and exploring. They're close to farm animals, pets, and wild animals. Instead of spending all day at school, they spend a few hours a week with Schools of the Air. Homework is due only once a week!

The Royal Flying Doctor Service's fleet of planes flies about 12,000,000 miles (20,000,000 km) every year.

Long-Distance Medical Care

Snakebites, motorcycle accidents, and heatstroke happen every day in the outback, but getting good medical care can be difficult. If someone needs to be rushed to a hospital, people can radio the Royal Flying Doctor Service (RFDS).

Most illnesses are easier to treat, though. Every farm and ranch has a kit of basic medicines, each identified by a number. For non-emergencies, people call the RFDS and describe their symptoms. Doctors working with the RFDS then prescribe the proper medicine by number.

Aborigines: Juggling Two Ways of Life

Most of Australia's Aborigines have been absorbed into white culture. But some live on Aboriginal reserves or in scattered towns in the outback. Tribal councils make important decisions for a group, and tribal elders are respected for their wisdom and spiritual insight.

A few Aboriginal groups live as they have for centuries. They live off the land, hunting with spears and woomeras (spear throwers) and gathering plants. Several clans sometimes meet in corroborees and perform traditional dances.

Aboriginal and Torres Strait Islander culture has experienced a revival in recent years. Every two years, indigenous groups gather at the Laura Festival on the Cape York Peninsula to celebrate their culture.

When Aborigines become sick, they seek modern medical care. But they often put more trust in their *ngangkari* than in the doctor. The ngangkari is part doctor and part priest. He or she understands the spiritual problem underlying an illness and performs rituals to relieve it.

Regaining their land rights has opened up more opportunities for Aborigines. Tourists in Australia often want to visit Aboriginal sites and observe Aboriginal arts and culture. In the past, non-Aborigines ran these tourist expeditions. Now some Aborigines are taking control of their own tours. Others work as guides or interpreters in national parks that are managed jointly by the Australian government and Aboriginal groups. This way, Aborigines can present their culture in an authentic way and protect their sacred sites.

Some Boomerangs Don't Come Back

Aborigines have used boomerangs for thousands of years. A boomerang is a crescent-shaped object carved from wood and often painted with animals and other designs. It can be used for hunting, fighting, or beating out dance rhythms. When thrown properly, it returns to the thrower. But boomerangs are not always designed to return. Some are just a type of hunting club. They drop to the ground after striking an animal. Cultures in India and Egypt also used curved hunting clubs, but only Australian Aborigines developed boomerangs that return.

More than a hundred kinds of fish are sold at the Sydney Fish Market. The colorful market is one of Sydney's top attractions.

Food from the Land

Cattle and sheep farms supply Aussies with plenty of beef and lamb. Chook (chicken) and pork are popular, too. Meat, potatoes, and vegetables make up a regular, everyday meal, but Australia's many immigrant communities spice up the basic fare. Big cities offer a tasty choice of Greek, Italian, Middle Eastern, Indian, Chinese, Japanese, Vietnamese, and Thai restaurants.

Australia abounds with seafood. Hundreds of species of fish from coastal waters end up on the table. Shark, whiting, and sea trout are favorites, as are shrimp, oysters, and enormous crayfish. Tasmanian crabs can weigh as much as 30 pounds (14 kg). Moreton Bay bugs are small and tasty crayfish.

How People Live **123**

An abundance of good food grows in Australia. Western Australia has famously sweet melons.

Fresh fruits are plentiful in Australia. Queenslanders are called banana-eaters because their state has so many banana trees. Other popular fruits include pineapples, paw-paws (papayas), mangoes, and passion fruit. They're eaten fresh, used in cooking, and made into fruit juices. Fruits from the bush include the quandong (a wild peach) and the native cherry of New South Wales.

Native wild animals find their way to the table, too. Emu meat is said to taste like turkey. Kangaroo meat is tender and low in cholesterol.

How to Eat Like an Aussie

A typical brekkie (breakfast) consists of eggs and snags (sausages). Hearty eaters prefer a plate of steak, pork chops, and snags. Snags cooked in egg batter are called toad in the hole. Lunch might be a sanger (sandwich) or fish and chips (french fries). But you must put malt vinegar on the chips. Tomato sauce (ketchup) goes on meat pies. A meat pie in pea soup or gravy is called a floater.

Looking for a snack? Go to a milk bar—that's a convenience store. If you want strong black tea, ask for "billy." Lemon squash is lemonade, icy poles are popsicles, and lollies are candy and sweets.

Traditionally, Australians ate a large breakfast of eggs and sausages. But these days, people are more likely to grab a bowl of cereal or a slice of bread.

Vegemite is Australia's multipurpose snack food. It's a gooey brown yeast-and-vegetable paste that's slightly softer than creamy peanut butter. Aussies spread Vegemite on bread, toast, and crackers. Even babies eat it as a "starter" food. Rich in B vitamins, it's good for cell growth, nerves, skin, and eyes.

Food for the Soul

"We'll throw another shrimp on the barbie for you," an Australian travel ad used to say. Barbies are a favorite social event. They can happen any time, any place. People barbecue at home, on the beach, in the bush, and in parks and picnic areas. Some restaurants and bars provide meat and let the customers grill it themselves.

The Story of Vegemite

Fred Walker knew that yeast was nutritious. He wanted his food company in Melbourne to make it in some delicious form. One day in 1922, Walker asked Dr. Cyril Callister, the company scientist, to come up with something. Callister brewed up a pasty mixture of yeast extract, celery, onions, and other ingredients. Walker held a competition to find a name for the new product, and the winner was "Vegemite." During World War II, Vegemite was part of soldiers' meals. It became so popular that, for a time, there was a Vegemite shortage. Vegemite-eating experts warn against eating it by the spoonful. Instead, spread butter on bread, smear Vegemite in with the butter, and enjoy!

With cities and suburbs becoming crowded, more people use their free time to "go bush." They spend a weekend or even a couple of weeks bushwalking—that is, hiking and camping in the bush. Some bushwalkers bring food with them, while others take the "survival" route. They hunt animals for food and cook them over a campfire.

Under the starry sky, the silence is enormous. The only sounds are the cries of wild things in the bush. Yet there are those who swear they hear more. Is it the song of a long-dead wanderer, or the murmurs of ancient spirits of the land? In Australia, anything is possible.

Australians love to get out into the bush, where they can relax and enjoy a campfire.

Fast Facts

Official name: Commonwealth of Australia

Capital: Canberra

Official language: English

Official religion: None

Sydney

Australia's flag

Russell Falls

National anthem:	"Advance Australia Fair"		
Government:	Constitutional monarchy		
Head of state:	The British monarch; in practice, the head of state is the governor-general, who performs functions in the monarch's absence.		
Head of government:	Prime minister		
Area:	2,978,146 square miles (7,713,364 sq km)		
Coordinates of geographic center:	27°00' S, 133°00' E		
Dimensions:	Australia measures almost 2,485 miles (4,000 km) from east to west and about 2,300 miles (3,700 km) from north to south.		
Bordering countries:	Indonesia lies to the northwest, across the Timor and Arafura seas; Papua New Guinea lies to the northeast, across the Torres Strait; to the southeast, across the Tasman Sea, is New Zealand; across the Indian Ocean to the south is the continent of Antarctica.		
Highest elevation:	Mount Kosciusko, 7,310 feet (2,228 m)		
Lowest elevation:	Lake Eyre, 52 feet (16 m) below sea level		

Average temperatures:

	January	July
Sydney	71.8°F (22.1°C)	53.2°F (11.8°C)
Darwin	83.3°F (28.5°C)	76.8°F (24.9°C)

Average annual rainfall:

Sydney	48 inches (122 cm)
Darwin	62 inches (157 cm)

National population (2006 est.): 20,636,000

Great Barrier Reef

Population of largest cities (2002 est):

Sydney	4,170,900
Melbourne	3,524,100
Brisbane	1,689,100
Perth	1,413,600
Adelaide	1,114,300

Famous landmarks:
- *Uluru, or Ayers Rock,* Yulara
- *Great Barrier Reef*
- *Sydney Opera House,* Sydney
- *Kakadu National Park,* Jabiru
- *Bungle Bungle Range,* Kununurra

Industry: Sheep and cattle ranching are important agricultural activities. Australia is the world's largest producer of wool, and beef products are important exports. Major crops include wheat, barley, grapes, sugarcane, sorghum, and oats. Australia is rich in minerals. It is the world's top producer of bauxite and is an important producer of coal, copper, diamonds, gold, iron, lead, and nickel. It is also the source of most of the world's opals. Most of Australia's manufacturing takes place in Victoria and New South Wales. Major factory products include processed foods, metals, machinery, cars, paper, chemicals, and clothing.

Currency: The basic unit of currency is the Australian dollar (A$), which is divided into one hundred cents. In 2006, A$1.00 was equal to US$0.74, and US$1.00 was equal to A$1.36.

Currency

System of weights and measures: Metric system

Literacy: 99 percent

Schoolchildren

Evonne Goolagong Cawley

Common Australian words and phrases:

barbie	barbecue
bikie	motorcycle rider
billabong	water hole in a dry riverbed
fair dinkum	really, honestly
g'day	hello
jumbuck	sheep
jumper	sweater
lollies	candy, sweets
mate	buddy, pal
sunbake	sunbathe
walkabout	long, rambling trip
water biscuit	cracker

Famous Australians:

Evonne Goolagong Cawley (1951–)
Tennis player

Russell Crowe (1964–)
Actor

Percy Grainger (1882–1961)
Composer

Steve Irwin (1962–2006)
Conservationist and televison star

Thomas Keneally (1935–)
Writer

Nicole Kidman (1967–)
Actor

Rupert Murdoch (1931–)
Media executive

Joan Sutherland (1926–)
Opera singer

Patrick White (1912–1990)
*Winner of 1973 Nobel Prize
for Literature*

To Find Out More

Nonfiction

▶ Arnold, Caroline. *Australian Animals*. New York: HarperCollins, 2000.

▶ Banting, Erinn. *Australia: The People*. New York: Crabtree, 2003.

▶ Cefrey, Holly. *Exploring Australia: Using Charts, Graphs, and Tables*. New York: PowerKids Press, 2004.

▶ Collard, Sneed B., and Robin Brickman (illustrator). *One Night in the Coral Sea*. Watertown, Mass.: Charlesbridge, 2005.

▶ Darlington, Robert. *Australia*. Austin, Tex.: Raintree/Steck-Vaughn, 2001.

▶ Kerns, Ann. *Australia in Pictures*. Minneapolis: Lerner, 2004.

▶ Lewin, Ted, and Betsy Lewin. *Top to Bottom Down Under*. New York: HarperCollins, 2005.

▶ Niz, Xavier. *Australia*. Mankato, Minn.: Capstone Press, 2006.

Fiction

▶ Baglio, Ben E. *Dolphin Diaries*. New York: Scholastic, 2003.

▶ Clarke, Judith. *Kalpana's Dream*. Asheville, N.C.: Front Street, 2005.

▶ Honey, Elizabeth, and William Clarke (illustrator). *Don't Pat the Wombat!* New York: Random House, 2001.

▶ Lindsay, Norman. *The Magic Pudding: Being the Adventures of Bunyip Bluegum and His Friends Bill Barnacle and Sam Sawnoff*. New York: New York Review of Books, 2004.

▶ West, Tracey. *The Outback: Survivor #4*. New York: Simon Spotlight, 2005.

Videos and DVDs

▶ *Australia: Land Beyond Time*. DVD. Razor Digital Entertainment, 2005.

▶ *Discovering Australia*. Video. Reader's Digest, 1997.

▶ *Indigenous Children in Australia*. Video and DVD. UN Social Studies School Service, 2003.

▶ *Touring Australia's Great National Parks*. Video. Questar, 2002.

Web Sites

▶ **About Australia**
http://www.australia.gov.au/about-australia
The Australian government's guide to the country's land, people, environment, sports, and many other subjects.

▶ **Time for Kids Specials**
http://www.timeforkids.com/TFK/specials/story/0,6079,53716,00.html
Australian kids discuss their lives and the activities they enjoy, as well as differences between Australia and the United States.

Organizations and Embassies

▶ **Australian High Commission to Canada**
50 O'Conner Street
Suite 710
Ottawa, Ontario K1P 6L2
613-236-0841
www.canada.embassy.gov.au/

▶ **Embassy of Australia**
1601 Massachusetts Avenue, NW
Washington, DC 20036-2273
202-797-3000
www.austemb.org

Meet the Author

ANN HEINRICHS fell in love with faraway places as a child while reading Doctor Dolittle books and *Peter Freuchen's Book of the Seven Seas*. As an adult, her travels have taken her through most of the United States and much of Europe, as well as Africa, the Middle East, and East Asia.

An editor for many years, Ann has conducted extensive research on Australia. As project editor for the World Heritage series, copublished by UNESCO and Children's Press, she helped develop English-language editions of *Australia: Land of Natural Wonders*, *Prehistoric Rock Art* (which included many Aborigine sites), and *Coral Reefs* (which included the Great Barrier Reef).

"For this book, I also interviewed several Australians about their experiences in the outback. I attended a didgeridoo performance, studied the journals of Captain James Cook, and paid zoo visits to kangaroos, koalas, wombats, emus, and pythons. And riding a camel in the Sinai desert gave me a feel for the camelback explorers of Australia's desert interior.

"Of course, much of my hard-core research happens at the library. When I begin a book, I head straight for the reference department. Some of my favorite resources are United Nations publications, *Europa World Yearbook*, and the periodicals databases."

Ann prefers writing nonfiction, rather than fiction. "I guess I'm a frustrated journalist," she says. "I'm driven to track down facts and present them in an engaging way. For me, facts are more exciting than fiction, and I want my readers to experience a subject as passionately as I do. Also, I feel it's vital for American kids to understand unfamiliar cultures, so I like to report on what kids in another country are doing—to tell about their interests, values, and daily lives, as well as their economic role in the family."

Ann grew up roaming the woods of Arkansas. Now, she lives in Chicago, Illinois. After pursuing successful careers as an editor and an advertising copywriter, she is now the author of more than two hundred books for children and young adults on American, European, Asian, and African history and culture. She holds bachelor's and master's degrees in piano performance. More recently, her performing arts have been t'ai chi empty-hand and sword forms. She is an award-winning martial artist and has participated in regional and national tournaments.

Photo Credits

Photographs © 2007:

age fotostock/Kevin Shafer: 19, 131

Alamy Images: 66, 91, 124, 126 (Bill Bachman), 81, 123 (Danita Delimont), 121 (Paul Dymond), 15 (North Wind Picture Archives), 2 (David Noton Photography), 125 (numb), 88, 133 top (Nicholas Pitt), 82 (Doug Steley), 8 (Penny Tweedie), 9 (Patrick Ward), 16 (Westend61), 58 top (John White Photos), 87 (Janine Wiedel Photolibrary), 22 (World Pictures Ltd.), 96 (World Religions Photo Library), 7 bottom, 100 (WorldFoto)

AP/Wide World Photos: 77 (Jennifer Graylock), 111 top (Tony Gutierrez), 55 (Itsuo Inouye), 26 (Vivien Jones)

Art Directors and TRIP Photo Library: 72, 132 bottom (Helene Rogers), 27 bottom, 45, 71 bottom, 127 (Robin Smith), 44 (Bob Turner), 37 (Joan Wakelin)

Art Resource, NY/Werner Forman: 98

Bridgeman Art Library International Ltd., London/New York: 53 (Giraudon/Archives Larousse, Paris, France), 47 (Ken Welsh/Private Collection)

Corbis Images: 21 (O. Alamany & E. Vicens), 67 (John Carnemolla/Australian Picture Library), 111 bottom (Duomo), 76 (Robert Garvey), 107 (Roger Garwood & Trish Ainslie), 85 (John Van Hasselt), 106, 122 (Dallas and John Heaton/Free Agents Limited), 71 top (Dave G. Houser), 95 (Roberto Melchiorre/zefa), 80, 92, 118 (Paul A. Souders), 56, 58 bottom, 64, 117 (Penny Tweedie), 89, 108 (John Van Hasselt/Sygma), 105 (Marcus Vetter)

Dembinsky Photo Assoc.: 10 (E.R. Degginger), 114 (Steve Robertson), 34, 35 bottom (Martin Withers)

Getty Images: 13 (John William Banagan/The Image Bank), 31 (Jonathan S. Blair/National Geographic), 102 top (ChinaFotoPress), 29 (Nicole Duplaix/National Geographic), 78 (Jason Edwards/National Geographic), 112, 133 bottom (Evening Standard/Hulton Archive), 39 (Gordon Gahan/National Geographic), 115 (Fraser Hall/Robert Harding World Imagery), 102 bottom (Frazer Harrison), 68 (Peter Hendrie/Photographer's Choice), 103 top (John Kobal Foundation/Hulton Archive), 110 bottom (Stephane L'Hostis), 103 bottom (Ethan Miller), 104 (Patrick Riviere), 101 (Eric Ryan), 109 (Terrence Spencer/Time Life Pictures), 113 (Pierre Tostee/ASP), 60 (Ian Waldie), 94 (Jonathon Wood)

Landov, LLC/Will Burgess/REUTERS: 62

MapQuest.com, Inc.: 57, 131 top

Mary Evans Picture Library: 48, 51

Masterfile: 14, 69, 116 (R. Ian Lloyd), 18 (Lloyd Sutton), 24 (Brian Sytnyk)

Minden Pictures: 40, 41, 132 top (Fred Bavendam), 38 (Jean-Paul Ferrero), 30 right, 42 (Michael & Patricia Fogden), cover, 6, 32, 36 (Mitsuaki Iwago), 43 top (Jean-Marc La Roque/Auscape), 33 (D. Parer & E. Parer-Cook/Auscape), 35 top (Mike Parry)

National Geographic Image Collection/Tim Laman: 30 left

National Library of Australia: 110 top (Portrait of A.B. Paterson, 1890, nla.pic-an22199070)

Nature Picture Library Ltd./Dave Watts: 20, 28

Photo Researchers, NY/Brian Brake: 97

photolibrary.com: 120 (Robert Harding Picture Library Ltd.), 75, 93

PictureQuest/Chris Jones: 43 bottom

Superstock, Inc.: 27 top, 74 (age fotostock), 11, 130 left (Prisma)

The Art Archive/Picture Desk: 49

TIPS Images/Harald Sund: 7 top, 23

www.Didjshop.com: 99

Maps and illustrations by XNR Productions, Inc.

EAST ORANGE PUBLIC LIBRARY

3 2665 0035 9596 6

j994 HEI
Heinrichs, Ann.
Australia